TOOLS MATTER
FOR PRACTICING
THE SPIRITUAL LIFE

TOOLS MATTER

— FOR —

PRACTICING

— THE —

SPIRITUAL LIFE

Mary Margaret Funk, O.S.B.

CONTINUUM

NEW YORK • LONDON

2001

The Continuum International Publishing Group Inc
370 Lexington Avenue, New York, NY 10017

The Continuum International Publishing Group Ltd
The Tower Building, 11 York Road, London SE1 7NX

Printed in the United States of America

Library of Congress Cataloging-in-Publication Data

Funk, Mary Margaret.
Tools matter for practicing the spiritual life / Mary Margaret Funk.
p. cm.
Includes bibliographical references.
ISBN 0-8264-1351-X (pbk.)
1. Spiritual life—Catholic Church. 2. Prayer. 3. Asceticism.
I. Title.
BV5031.2 .F86 2001
248.4'6—dc21
2001042149

CONTENTS

PREFACE

Thoughts Matter (Continuum, 1998) was my first attempt to retrieve and reclaim the wisdom tradition of the desert elders. The classic eight thoughts (food, sex, things, anger, dejection, acedia, vainglory, pride) that John Cassian wrote about in his *Institutes* and *Conferences* require practical tools for the serious seeker. In this second book, I have extracted those tools and found enhanced teachings about them that were lived out during later centuries, for example, the cell, fasting, manual labor, and ceaseless prayer. This book, *Tools Matter,* does what *Thoughts Matter* did but with practice rather than thoughts. I found more than twenty-five practices that can be reappropriated today as tools to assist the contemplative seeker. This book is for those of us seeking spiritual direction.

Meg Funk
Feast of St. Benedict 2001

ACKNOWLEDGMENTS

Deo Gratias, I hope you can see the fruit of your collaboration:
Mary Sue Freiberger, O.S.B., Carol Falkner, O.S.B., and my Benedictine
sisters at Beech Grove, Sharon Richardt, D.C., and the St. Vincent
Hospital of Indianapolis Associates at Seton Cove, the Monastic Spiritual
Direction Institute at Benedict Inn, the Trappist Formation Directors at
New Melleray, Iowa, Benedictines of Clyde, Bruno Barnhart, O.S.B. Cam.,
Columba Stewart, O.S.B., Monastic Interreligious Dialogue Board and
Advisors, Jim and Marina Funk, Carolyn Benner, Laura Klauberg, Evelyn
Friedman, Kate Olson, Jack Ryan, Toddy Daly, Jeanne Knoerle, S.P.,
Dorothy Bass and the Lilly Endowment, Cathy Selin, Colleen Mathews,
Frank Oveis and the Continuum International Publishing Group.

INTRODUCTION

A Garden Where Tools Matter

Tools Matter. In the garden of our souls we are both the farmer and the seed. We've been planted. Our awakening experience has happened. Staying awake is the problem. Our soil soon becomes crowded with weeds. If we know ourselves, we know that one disorienting factor can obliterate any peak experience in the blink of an eye. We try to pray but our thoughts are like weeds that choke the good seed. Sometimes we feel as if we were going mad, that we are out of our minds. Perhaps we should want to be "out of our mind" because our thoughts are always conditioned to keep us in stale, starched patterns.

How can we tend the garden of our souls? Are there any tools? How do these tools work? This book is a brief presentation of tools found in the Christian tradition and how they worked for the early monks and nuns. These monastics were people like you and me. They felt the same impulse we do—they needed help. To find that help, they went to visit the early hermits, quiet dwellers in the desert, and asked them, "How do you do it?" "How can I do it?" These wise persons taught them to guard their hearts, to watch their thoughts, to spend time in vigils, to fast, to confess, to practice ceaseless prayer, to practice the prayer of the heart, and to do manual labor, to name a few of the recommended practices.

Since the fifth century, variations and invented tools have been added by those who have gone before us: the "Little Way," the practice of abandonment, the practice of the presence, the practice of emptiness, recollection, colloquy, the practice of no preference, and suffering as a practice. No one needs all these practices, but it is helpful to know about these hallowed paths in our Christian tradition.

A critical assumption in this book is found in John Cassian's notion of "springing up" (*Inst.* 4.43).[1] From this important text in Cassian's *Institutes* we see that there is a sequence to the inner journey. The first thing required is a disposition of reverence, of awe toward God, a disposition that fosters compunction and humility. But the actual work of the spirit is, somewhat surprisingly, a reversal of our ordinary intuition. We assume that we must learn and practice the virtue of humility and strive to put love into practice. This is not the advice that stretches over Cassian's eight *Institutes* and into his first eight *Conferences*. We need not assert "love." It just happens when we remove the weeds.

Presuming that we have left our former way of life, we are told simply and humbly to remove the obstacles to prayer. We are told to weed our garden. The obstacles (weeds) are the eight thoughts (later translated into the seven capital sins): thoughts of food, sex, things, anger, dejection, acedia, vaingory, and pride. In practice, the way to purity of heart, and hence to having a full-flowered garden, is to remove the human "weeds" by reducing, redirecting, and removing our thoughts. Then God's presence "springs up." We experience God (knowledge and contemplation). So, right effort is to weed, not plant.

God's work is prayer and our work is "un-thinking." This wisdom of the desert fathers and mothers is simply to remain in God's presence and, when thoughts rise, to redirect them. Our only effort is to let thoughts simply be and to refrain from giving our attention to our thoughts. Those same desert dwellers teach us many ways to do this. This book is a collection of their teachings on "right effort" that puts into practice ways to lay aside our thoughts so that love (the consciousness of God) can spring up.

As difficult as this must sound to beginners, it is also sweet. It asks for a single-minded attention to our thoughts with no commentary or clutter in our minds. This is a liberating experience and we soon fall into the mystery of hearing the still, small voice awakening to the subtle presence of God in our everyday experience. This practice calls for no wild seeking of exotic people, places, or things. We simply understand that the reign of God is already blooming within us.

Some might say that this presence can be felt without inner work. Many, if not all, of us have had the experience of a breakthrough of the transcendent. But because of our human condition, in a short time the memory of such an encounter vanishes and no sustained vigor with its quickened warmth is left in our hearts. "Now what?" says the mind and the body to the soul. The answer from the monastic tradition is to learn to observe and control our thoughts. To do this we use the tools the early monks and nuns found helpful as long ago as the fourth century.

We find those teachings in Cassian's works where he makes an extraordinary discovery about the nature of our minds.

> Therefore, before we pray we should make an effort to cast out from the innermost parts of our heart whatever we do not wish to steal upon us as we pray, so that in this way we can fulfill the apostolic words: "Pray without ceasing." And: "In every place lift up pure hands without anger and dissension." For we shall be unable to accomplish this command unless our mind, purified of every contagion of vice and given over to virtue alone as to a natural good, is fed upon the continual contemplation of almighty God. (*Conf.* 9.3.4)

> For the character of the soul is not inappropriately compared to a very light feather or plume. If it has not been harmed or spoiled by some liquid coming from the outside, thanks to its inherent lightness it is naturally borne to the heavenly heights by the slightest breath. But if it has been weighed down by a sprinkling or an outpouring of some liquid, not only will it not be borne off by its natural lightness and snatched up into the air, but it will even be pressed down to the lowest places on the earth by the weight of the liquid that it has taken on. (*Conf.* 9.4.1)
>
> Likewise, if our mind has not been burdened by the worldly vices and concerns that assail it and been spoiled by the liquid of a harmful wantonness, it will be lightened by the natural goodness of its purity and be lifted up to the heights by the subtlest breath of spiritual meditation. Leaving behind low and earthly places, it will

be carried away to heavenly and invisible ones. Hence we are rightly warned by the precepts of the Lord: "See that your hearts not be weighted down by surfeiting and drunkenness and worldly concerns." (*Conf.* 9.4.2)

Therefore, if we wish our prayers to penetrate not only the heavens but even what is above the heavens, we should make an effort to draw our mind, purged of every earthly vice and cleansed of all the dregs of the passions, back to its natural lightness, so that thus its prayer might ascend to God, unburdened by the weight of any vice. (*Conf.* 9.4.3)

This long quote from Cassian tells us that by nature we are good. We have an inner quality of soul that is as light as a feather. Our "right effort" is simply and consistently to remove the obstacles to letting our inner nature rise. His is an optimistic view rather than a negative or harsh one. The practices he suggests actually work, and if we follow them, thoughts no longer obscure our awareness of God.

Just as our "thoughts matter" we see that "tools matter," too. Most beginners require tools to notice their thoughts and start the inner work. Early on the journey, we notice that when our thoughts are stilled pure prayer arises. There are many books about prayer and there are many books of prayer. This is a book about those tools we can take from the early Christian tradition to do this inner work so pure prayer happens. We have teachings from our desert elders that help us understand how this garden of our souls is nurtured and then flourishes.

1

❦

THOUGHTS AND TOOLS

When the hermits left their towns and dwelled in their desert caves, cells, or temporary shelters, they found that their physical environment heightened not only their desire for God but also their drag into sin. They couldn't sustain their resolve. You would think that leaving family, possessions, and occupations would free the body, mind, and soul for prayer. Not so. Leaving their previous modes of life reversed their external ways of being but their internal ways of being—memory, imagination, and rational thinking—only became more aggravated in isolation. Therefore, in the desert these seekers took up a new inner work: thoughts.

Teachings on Thoughts and Practice

We, who are contemplatives in the world, can benefit from how the desert elders trained their minds. We need to enter into their Neo-Platonic mindset to understand the theory and then to translate it into contemporary terms.

Greek anthropology holds that persons have a body, a mind that enlivens the body, and a soul that puts a life force in the body and the mind, that is eternal and real. In the cosmos, they believed, there was a collective soul. Christian thinkers in late antiquity appropriated this grid and baptized it.[1] They said: the Holy Spirit, the soul of our soul, enlivens the body, mind, and soul given to each human person.[2] The cosmic Christ is the collective soul. The most exalted work that humans can aspire to is contemplation. No being of a lower life form can do that and know that they are doing it.

The gift of being human is a faculty or a capacity to be aware of our thoughts. In this awareness, we can observe that thoughts come and then go; we can distinguish ourselves from our thoughts. We are not our thoughts. We have thoughts, said our desert ancestors, over and over in many ways, beginning the long philosophical debate over objectivity and subjectivity. But even if we are not our thoughts, we must deal with them. Thoughts come again and again. But if a thought is not "thought about" or accompanied by another thought the thought will go away. If another thought, sustained with attention, accompanies the first thought, then the thought thickens and forms into feelings or emotions. If those feelings and emotions coalesce into desires, they become dense and evolve into passions. Passions (still passive) rise strong, hard, and fast. They quicken the mind and pose a question: to consent or not to consent? To consent to good thoughts or desires or passions becomes a virtue, or the habit of doing good. To consent to bad thoughts or desires or passions becomes a vice or a sin, a habit of doing wrong. Good is beneficial to the soul and vices are destructive to it. Some thoughts come into consciousness already as an emotion since they rise so quickly we don't note the signals at their first "rising." Awareness of our thoughts allows distance from them which is the first step in discernment.

Hermits were initiated into the nuances of the mind. They learned, sometimes the hard way, that to overcome a passion was more difficult than to overcome a thought. At the level of a thought, when an impression is young, new, just springing up, there is supple agility. At the level of desire, there is a struggle to reduce, redirect, or react to the feeling. At the intensity of a full blown passion, the energies are so thick that holding one's own is almost impossible. Monastics put these insights into teachings about temptations, demons, and thoughts, but the patterns are universal and apply to all of us. The sooner we notice a thought and take appropriate action, the easier is the response. We can see why the hermits challenged themselves to "keep vigilant." Practice is the work of attention, of keeping awake.

There are no isolated thoughts. The Greek word for thought is *logismos,* which means "train of thoughts." Thoughts are like a comet that has a life of its own with a trail of little vapors in its tail. Therefore, the way to master thoughts is to notice them early, often, and consistently and to respond to them deliberately. This is the underlying reason why a practice is helpful—some elders would say, even essential—for the spiritual life.

It's helpful to beginners to see that there are eight clusters of thoughts. Thoughts cluster around the themes of food, sex, things, anger, dejection, acedia, vainglory, and pride.[3] Universally, it seems, we all have the same experience. These thoughts rise in everyone, at all times and in all places. Some traditions give these thoughts other names, but the content and even the progression are the same.

There is a system to our thoughts. The first three thoughts (food, sex, and things) are afflictions of the body; the second ones (anger and dejection) are afflictions of the mind; and the third ones (acedia, vainglory, pride) are afflictions of the soul. The system has a logical sequence and makes for sound teaching.

Thoughts have another degree of gravity when they become "second thoughts," or intentions. For example, though one might have an affliction about food, the thought is not usually about food, it is about "self" and one's motivation. We call these thoughts "second thoughts," and we say that our thoughts *about* thoughts matter more than the thoughts themselves. This gets tricky but it makes a good deal of difference: to eat is a behavior we share in common with the animal world, but to be mindful while eating is contemplative work.

The Greeks also examined the sources of thoughts. Where do they come from? The elders soon sorted them from their fruits. Some thoughts rise from my own memories, desires, or experiences that are stored in consciousness. Some thoughts are from God and are inspirations of the Holy Spirit. Other thoughts are from evil sources outside of myself. The demons seem to know us well and sink into any vulnerable crevice of weakness. We can look at our thoughts and recognize their source. If a thought is from God, we need to cultivate it. If it is from ourselves, we need to check it because we know we are by nature good, but conditioned. We experience ignorance of the good, a weak will, and an inclination toward evil. This is the teaching stored in the myth of original sin.

Everyone can have the experience of being a contemplative. We must simply slow down our thoughts, still ourselves. When our thinking subsides, so does our consciousness of self, and when that happens, the "I" of the mind's eye mirrors God. We are at rest. This rest is the enjoyment of full consciousness, and when the "I" is not driving the self into ego-attention, God's action and God's direction can take over and enfold us. Whether this is for a split second or longer, this depth marks the soul indelibly. Often in our ordinary lives love springs up. St. Benedict talks about an enlarged or dilated heart. Work, he says, is prayer and prayer is work. The effort is effortless but the love abides forever. The practices we will present in this book are natural and sustain a lifetime of loving.

But I'm getting ahead of our story. To get to this point we must attend to our thoughts. Are we thinking about food, or sex, or things? Are we in various stages of anger or depression? Our way of thinking shows us our consciousness. The contemplative prefers Christ. It's tragic to leave all, go to the desert—and then think about food for a lifetime. Not only in eternal life, but now, Christ promised, we can abide in God. We can become Christ conscious. We can't "think God," but what we can do is "un-think" other thoughts and let God spring up.

This un-thinking is orthopraxis, or right practice, just as orthodoxy is right belief. In orthopraxis we do our interior work as individuals. Is this work too self-centered? Ought we to serve others as the best use of our time? Zeal is essential to a healthy group, but this health requires that each individual come to the work of the group with readiness. Personal discipline has no substitute. Without good motivations and clear-sightedness, the group becomes simply a herd and its actions can easily become oppressive, closed-minded, and even a cult. I can only change myself. To change a group each person must undergo personal transformation. The starting point for community growth is the individual. The locus of consent is my thoughts.

Thus, we are back to *Thoughts Matter,* and when I notice my thoughts I must practice redirecting any thoughts that remove and distance me from my experience of God.

Lectio Divina

This Latin term *lectio divina* in its literal translation means "reading God." The Bible for Christians is the hallowed means to meet God because God is mediated through Scripture. The practice of *lectio divina* is like a tool bench or a shed next to the garden that stores the tools. It's the most important prayer practice because it is through Scripture that one personally enters into Christ through the life of Jesus, his teachings, his works, and his impact on others.

A functional definition of *lectio divina* is that it is an encounter between God and the human person. This encounter happens when the individual meets God in Scripture, and through the power of the four senses of Scripture, that person's spiritual senses of sight, sound, taste, touch, and smell encounter God's transcendence and God's immanence. So, we can say our human senses are dilated, expanded, even transcended to receive God. The medium is literature that transcends the literal level and penetrates meaning with symbol and grace, then returns to the literal, first level of discourse, and meets God. This literal encounter isn't the God "of faith" but the God "of experience."

Through the tool of *lectio divina,* we can literally "know" God and enter into a relationship just as we do with our friends. There are many communal prayer forms, like the Divine Office or the Eucharistic Liturgy, but the classic individual prayer form is *lectio divina.* What is so compelling about *lectio divina* as a prayer form is that its model of friendship between God and the soul is interactive. We have built-in spiritual senses to enable us to enter into this relationship. However, these senses need training and work to mature. *Lectio divina* is the kind of interactive experience that takes us to the deepest levels of contemplation.

The great saints often demonstrated the fruit of their *lectio.* Benedict in his seven-thousand-word Rule quotes Scripture three hundred times; St. Teresa of Avila quotes Scripture six hundred times; and St. John of the Cross quotes Scripture in his nine hundred pages of writings nine hundred times. Clearly, the transmission of God has come to us through God's word abiding in Scripture.

At the risk of failing to hand on this tradition in its entirety, I'd like to share some ways of practicing *lectio*.

A hermit who has lived twenty years in a thick woods in the Ozarks has his large Bible on a wooden stand to the right of his firm, upright chair that is made for study and attention. He does *lectio continua . . .* just reads slowly, ever so slowly, day after day, each page of the Old Testament, then each page of the New Testament in sequence until finished, and then the next day starts again from Genesis to the Book of Revelation. His bright, clear eyes dance when he describes his most recent "find" in Scripture.

Another monk, who lives by the sea, doesn't know how he does it. He reports that he just fell in love with Scripture. It shows! He can recite from memory the New Testament and has great facility for referencing the Hebrew Scriptures. He'll tell you, if you ask how to get started, just to start reading and when you get to a "hot spot" stay and linger. Go wherever it takes you. His specialty is the unitive sense of Scripture and he's developed structurally sound ways of interpreting the New Testament using a mandala. This love affair has taken him into literature, the Greek and Aramaic languages, as well as poetry—all manner of poetry.

A solitary who dwells in a city does *lectio* from the liturgical cycle in the eucharistic lectionary. She does homework on the text, usually just the Gospel reading, though in Advent and Lent she includes the Old Testament selection. She finds the root words in Greek or Hebrew and attends to a word or phrase throughout the day. She never spends less than thirty minutes a day on the next day's readings. Liturgy is her daily bread and her contact with the community. Her ears are ready and her heart is eager to be nourished. When asked if she ever uses an inspired text other than Sacred Scripture, she says she has no desire to do so, that her practice is to attend "in faith" to the transforming presence of Christ in Scripture.

A sister of my community teaches *lectio divina* to her seniors at a high school in Indianapolis, using the Sunday readings. One of her students wrote: "We have been practicing the prayer form of *lectio divina* for the past sixteen weeks. Every Friday we read the upcoming Sunday Gospel.

Our teacher reads the Gospel to us three times. She gives us a few minutes in between to think about the word of God. We then write down key words or phrases that have touched us in one way or another. After we have written the words down, we write a short reflection about what we think God is saying to us through the Scriptures." He goes on to say, in a letter written to the local archbishop (an assignment), "This is a very quiet and sacred time. Sometimes, sister plays quiet instrumental music while we reflect and write our meditation down in our journals. If it isn't too dark we turn the lights out and light a scented candle to set the mood. It's a very peaceful time. It is a time that I look forward to each week because I feel closer to God during this time of prayer."[4]

There are other practitioners who edify. Some who practice centering prayer do *lectio* either before or after their "sit." Father Thomas Keating recommends the practice of *lectio* after sitting so the mind is receptive and less active during meditation time.[5]

Some persons go through the four stages outlined in Guigo II's *Ladder*—*lectio, meditatio, oratio,* and *contemplatio*—when they do *lectio divina*.[6] *Lectio divina* is a personal prayer and each individual needs to see how it works best.

Beginners need simply to start. Take Scripture or an inspired text like *The Cloud of Unknowing*.[7] Keep the book in your room ready for *lectio divina. Lectio* is to be done when you are not doing anything else. It should be constantly in your mind, in your environment, so keep the book open, ready, handy, "at work." Do it every day and sometimes several times a day. It is not something ever to "get done." Do it all the time! Even in a monastic rhythm, no two days are alike. What is set is simply the schedule of the group. Our personal prayer is everything else. If we have little "reading" time, we can use the in-between times for thinking about the text. Praying without ceasing helps keep the mind receptive. Few of us can be hermits and most of us can't be monastics, but all of us have some discretionary time in our twenty-four-hour day. When we get accustomed to following the inspiration of the text, linger and let the dynamic of the sacred writing move you. The book used for *lectio divina* should be right there inviting us to another visit. When someone asks us what we are doing for *lectio,* we have a response ready, they can see it in our eyes. Here's a sample schedule for doing *The Cloud of Unknowing*.

1. Week One: Read the introduction slowly and deliberately. Survey each chapter. Read some commentary about this fourteenth-century book by an unknown author. Also read about the apophatic tradition of Christianity: about Gregory of Nyssa, John of the Cross, St. Thérèse of Lisieux, for instance.
2. Week Two: Read the entire text in sequence (ideally, during a retreat weekend).
3. Week Three: Begin again, reading the text somewhat slower; leisurely.
4. Week Four: Continue and finish the book of seventy-four chapters.
5. Second Month: Begin again and read slowly, stopping at a "hot spot" (something that catches the eye and warms the heart). Practice the recommended action that the text describes: take a word and lay it gently on a thought of God that rises toward the Cloud of Unknowing; or lay your word on thoughts that rise from daily life, putting them beneath the Cloud of Forgetting.
6. Continue the third reading for six months. During an ordinary day this practice will keep the teachings of the text in the mind.
7. Manifest to an "elder" how this practice is going. Share any obstacles in the way of the practice.
8. Continue the practice for a lifetime, but let the text change from time to time. All inspired texts are either Scripture or based on Scripture. Remember *lectio divina* is reading God!

Lectio divina is an appropriate way to read Scripture because God inspires these texts and there are many, many levels of meaning. Just as we have various physical senses so that we may perceive and receive reality, so Scripture has various senses to help readers understand the meaning of the text and reveal its encounter with God.

Traditionally there are four senses of Scripture, or four ways to read Scripture. Few Scripture passages lend themselves to using all four senses. Since Scripture mediates God for us, we need to stand before it listening with the ear of our hearts. Traditionally *lectio divina* uses only two: the literal sense and the symbolic or hidden sense.

We study the literal text in a prayerful way, using available tools of interpretation. To do this we analyze the text, the footnotes, the annotations, the introduction, and so on. The goal of such a study is to know what is being said. We try as much as possible to get at the intended meaning of the writer(s). This study-time may take a week, a month, or even longer. If we can afford the time and are attracted to the original languages, there is a great return on the investment of using them to see the subtle differences and major repetitions of themes that recur through Scripture.

The second sense or way to read Scripture is to seek out the symbolic, or hidden, meaning, which is carried along by the more obvious literal meaning. This is the meaning intended specifically for the prayerful reader. There are three kinds of possible hidden meanings: the first is the *allegorical* or the Christ-sense. To get at this meaning we take time to meditate, muse, wonder, stay with, and think about the word or experience. We think, feel, and stay with the "it" of the literal meaning. It is more than just reading Christ back into the text, it is allowing the Holy Spirit to guide us and inspire us with understanding. The ancients memorized most of the New Testament and all of the Psalms. Putting the words in our heart in this way makes the words portable and able to be retrieved when we are working, walking, resting, and thinking.

The second symbolic meaning is its dynamic or *moral* sense. This meaning is not so much simply found within the text as it is found by coming to the text by living into its meaning. This way of reading is beyond thinking. It asks us to absorb the meaning and appropriate it in our actual day. We pick up the burden of the text in our lives. The goal is to become Christ, become the Word, as St. Paul recommends. Then God is mediated through us.

For *lectio divina* to be effective, it is critical that we stay faithful to our vocation. We simply can't go one way with our feet and another with our heart. If we return to our former way of life in our external literal way of living, there is no possible benefit to the soul of the hidden or spiritual encounter with God that comes with *lectio divina*. Often in teaching centering prayer, I discover that some practitioner is having great difficulty staying awake or keeping up with designated practice time. In listening to them, I find that there's some serious attachment or relationship that is apart from their vowed life or an ambition that is not mindful of the poor. When this is the case, it's probably best to stop any pretext of *lectio divina,* go to confession, and attend to an external life of balance and harmony. A practice of *lectio* will emerge again from a deeper and heart-felt place when "walk" and "talk" are together.

To get at the inner dynamism of the word/event/experience, you must "act" it. This is an essential moment of *lectio divina.* To hear the word we must remove the obstacles and relate to the word/event/experience, as God becomes our reality. The literalness of the text drops off at this moment and the relationship is mediated through prayer and asceticism. Primarily, the obstacles to relating to God are removed by refraining from the eight thoughts, thereby allowing our relationship with God to be expressed through the prayer rising in our consciousness.

Because this dynamic moment of *lectio divina* pervades our whole life, there's no sequence that orders this prayer. But we cannot move to the goal of sacred reading if we are not *doing* the word. We must truly live into the text. All wisdom literature was lived first, then written. So, too, with us. We will understand the Scriptures only when we live them. This dynamic opens us to the moral sense of Scripture. It's not from the outside as an imposed "law," but an impulse from the deepest regions stored in our soul. It's like a physical cleansing that purifies our receptive system when our walk is the same as our talk. Then we *see* truth wherever it is to be found. This walk and talk isn't the same as the first renunciation of sin; this is the subtle behavior that matches the walk with the talk of specific understandings of Scripture study. An example of this would be if we entered into the text of "remain in me as I am in you" of John 15:4. We'd literally take up a prayer mantra or practice of the presence that keeps our thoughts centered on Christ.

Lectio divina is a way of living. There are many proofs that a person who is virtuous can understand and teach the Word better than a scholar can. However, if you do not know the literal meaning of the text first, you run the risk of bringing your own agenda to it and not receiving God's intended message. When you are aware of both the literal and symbolic sense of the texts, your prayer becomes dynamic and active. Your words and deeds close gaps in your everyday life.

Twining the literal and symbolic, or hidden, sense of Scripture will draw us into its *mystical* meaning. In the *unitive,* or mystical, sense of Scripture, we simply are receptive to the gift. There is no "right effort" we can use to obtain the experience of union with God. It is given to us by grace alone. We experience something new within the light that we have not seen before. There's brilliance, then, in that new light that moves to even greater brilliance: clear light. This is called *anagogical* (leading upward) since we move from light to light. Sometimes we move into the *teleological* (end) sense, or eschatological domain, of Scripture, since it deals with the final Reign of God. It can just be a hunch, a glimpse, or an inkling of something deeper here than meets the eye, but we know it when it happens. It's more certain than mathematics but more subtle than a cloudy day.

When we experience the unitive sense of Scripture we wait: all our active practices become stilled or passive for a time. Our practices move deeper too. If our way of ceaseless prayer is the Jesus prayer, then it shifts down to the prayer of the heart. If we've practiced living in the presence, it becomes an abiding method-less method. Our emptiness prayer becomes dazzling darkness or the Little Way, and colloquy becomes Christ consciousness. No one needs all these practices. Any one of them will lead us to the Center. I'm getting ahead of our story, but we can see the harmony here between *lectio divina* and our practice of particular ceaseless prayer. Basically we have replaced our afflictions with dispositions that accompany *lectio divina.*

For some, especially for those who prefer an apophatic path, the path of imageless prayer, there is a natural affinity to a meditation/contemplative sitting practice like centering prayer or Christian meditation practice. To sit, contemplate, and taste silence in a profound ever-deepening practice of meditation becomes a habit, even when it is difficult. This kind of practice has immense benefits for daily life. It incorporates the dynamic sense of *lectio divina* and facilitates an abiding consciousness of God. This leads one naturally to do ascetic practices, since no thought other than God is attractive.

For others the Jesus Prayer, having become the prayer of the heart, brings them to an inner stillness, aloneness before God. Others begin with colloquy before the Blessed Sacrament and are taken into wordless resting between times of mindfulness. All these practices will be considered in subsequent chapters.

More important than how we do *lectio divina* and what *lectio divina* is, is that we do it. We let God direct it and what emerges instructs us about what it is. *Lectio divina* is the nourishment that fuels ceaseless prayer.

What if I'm not attracted to Scripture? Some individuals, especially women, find it violent, sexist, too academic, and full of memories of childhood catechism or family malformation. Scripture isn't a helpful starting point for many people today.

There is also *lectio* of experience or *lectio* of nature. Let's take an ordinary scene on the back porch. I drink a cup of coffee there each morning. It's important that this method of *lectio* be method-less insofar as we don't do the four movements in a single "sit." It takes months. But there is strenuous effort in (a) keeping the time sacred, (b) doing nothing else during that time, and (c) restraining the mind from other thoughts. This practice of *lectio* is very close to the recollection taught by St. Teresa of Avila. It's obvious that she did this kind of *lectio divina* during her travels. Another example of the *lectio* of nature is Julian of Norwich's famous meditation on a hazelnut.

After this phase of effort, there is a joy and an attraction that prevail and *lectio* becomes natural and a way of being in the world, or a way of being in the monastery with images, stories, words of wisdom, connecting with sight, sound, smell, touch, and taste. *Lectio divina* becomes the culture or the way of life that protects, expresses, and brings to fullness our vocation. In this sense we are all monastics. Our cell is our heart. God calls us. We return to our heart's desire.

John Cassian's Four Renunciations

We must resist any path that leads us away from our heart's desire. We are made for God and we have profound, ready-made inclinations toward God. The good news is that this desire, when fulfilled, is also in our best self-interest. However, the mysterious direction we must go is through the door of the four renunciations; this teaching is from John Cassian. The teaching on the tools begins but does not end with Cassian. For those who don't know Cassian, I'd like to introduce you to him. John Cassian was born in the 360's in Dobrudja, a part of modern-day Romania. He was classically trained in Latin and Greek. He left for Palestine around 380 and settled in a monastery in Bethlehem. Like many seekers of his time, inspired by the lives of the desert fathers and mothers of Egypt, he was not content merely to hear stories about famous ascetics but went to meet them himself. In a wonderfully ingenious collection, he wrote down the teachings of thousands of solitaries in the early Christian era who lived in the deserts of Egypt, Syria, and Palestine. He left for Egypt in the mid 380's and spent about fifteen years there, settling as a monk at Scetis in the Wadi al-Natrum. He probably left Egypt around 399–400 because of the Origenist controversy and ended up in Constantinople. Cassian was probably ordained to the deaconate before 403 when John Chrysostom was bishop. He traveled to Rome after St. John Chrysostom's exile on account of the Nestorian controversy. We don't know much about him from 405–413. Perhaps he was in Antioch or Bethlehem, or he may have remained in Rome. We do know that he founded two monasteries in Marseille in the mid 410's, one for monks and one for nuns. He died in the mid 430's.[8]

Because his work was in Latin and not in Greek his writings got a permanent place two hundred years later in the Rule of Benedict. John Cassian wrote two major works and one minor treatise: twelve *Institutes* and twenty-four *Conferences* and seven books *On the Incarnation of the Lord, Against Nestorius*. His feast is celebrated on February 29th in the Orthodox Church.

Cassian was a student of Evagrius, a Greek scholar/mystic, who was in turn influenced by the great Scripture exegete Origen of Alexandria. This important group of monastic theologians built upon each other's teachings, frequently using the image of a journey to describe the spiritual life. This journey, they taught, required four renunciations. The first: to transform our ordinary, external human journey into a spiritual one. This renunciation has two phases. The first phase is to follow our baptismal call to turn away from Satan, from works of evil, from any good that is not God and any self that is not for others. This first phase teaches us to imitate Christ and to belong to the ecclesial community described in the Acts of the Apostles. The second phase of the first renunciation encourages us to renounce "ways of life" that lead away from the spiritual or the hidden life.

Sometimes this first renunciation takes the form of entering a monastery or changing our job or making or breaking a relationship. It may include an effort to surround ourselves with a culture that supports our choices. This effort may include renouncing our family of origin, some of our friends, the joy of having children, status and rank, or entitlements that provide us desirable opportunities. We might renounce property, possessions, and even professions. We often are asked to renounce a personal "mission" for the sake of a community mission or another selfless call. In short we renounce our former way of life.

By our former way of life, we mean all the ways we have lived externally: our family, profession, status, class, possessions, education, identity-bound origins like being Irish, American, Hoosier, or feminist Catholic. All of these culturally condition our being and must be renounced as controlling mechanisms. This conversion from the control of our former life for the sake of a noble call is what we call the first renunciation.

Notice that usually our former way of life isn't one of sin or decadence. It's a good surrendered for the sake of another good. It goes without saying that if we live a "bad sort of life" we would have to exercise great diligence to lay aside sinful ways and patterns before the first renunciation can even begin. The purpose of this renunciation is to begin to lift up our body, mind, and soul to God and to move away from controlling, self-willed projects. These works, no matter how beneficial they may be to others, simply shore up our ego and make our own personality our main concern in life. This renunciation is required of all baptized persons. Over the centuries, this first renunciation became confused with giving up one's ways of sin, but the real burden of the first renunciation is more positive than negative—to shift into God's way.

From the outside, we often can't tell if our neighbor has made that first renunciation because it looks so ordinary. In fact, maybe he or she shifted from the single life to marriage and family or from self-employment in business to a service-oriented, worker-class job because of God's prompting. Or maybe our neighbor has moved from a bedroom community of a large city to a housing district made up of lower-income families for explicit work with the underserved. This shift from our former way of life may have no external signs, yet internally it is a relinquishing of our old way for a new way of being toward God and others. We may embrace the facts of our former way because of necessity, such as a profession or external symbols of power, but we strive to do it with detachment and attention to our hidden spiritual journey.

Our path may simply be to "have no attachment" and to abandon ourselves to God's way as St. Paul did after his conversion.

This leads to the second renunciation, which has two phases also. First we notice our thoughts, not just our external actions, deeds, or surroundings. In this phase of the spiritual journey, we decide to let go of attachment to any thoughts that controlled us in our former way of life. This second renunciation leads us to an interior life of chaste thinking. The second phase of this renunciation is to look not only at our thoughts but also at our motivations and intentions. We have tools for this work.

In John Cassian's Third Conference: *On Renunciation,* attributed to Abba Paphnutius, we read: "Therefore, if we desire to achieve true perfection we ought to strive so that, just as with our body we have disdained parents, homeland, wealth, and pleasures of the world, we may also in our heart abandon all these things and not turn back again in our desires to what we have left behind, like those who were led out [of Egypt] by Moses" (*Conf.* 3.7.5).

The desert abbas and ammas discovered that it wasn't enough to leave their former way of life. They found that their thoughts, desires, and passions followed them to their caves. They remembered their relationships, diet, possessions, status, climate, and personal comforts. Their past hurts, when remembered years later, conjured up the same and even more intense anger and depression. Even the good that they did fed into their fantasies. Remembering their past with embellishment quickly became entangled with vainglory and waxed into full-blown pride when they took all the credit, and they even imagined doing lewd deeds because of anticipated pleasure.

All of this means that, though we leave behind our former way of life, there may still live in our hearts desires that are not in harmony with living toward God. We may not live exteriorly as we did before, but if that life is still held in the mind's eye, eventually we will take back what we've given up when, faced with temptations, we discover our weakness of resolve.

The book *Thoughts Matter* is about this second renunciation. Most of us will be at work on this purgative stage for our entire lifetime. The interior life is not achieved by simply withdrawing physically from our former way of life. Perhaps the biggest danger is becoming stuck in our new life with old patterns of mindless living, unconscious that we have thoughts at all! The classic eight thoughts—of food, sex, things, anger, dejection, acedia, vainglory, and pride—follow us. If our former life is still living and breathing in our hearts, not only is there no benefit from leaving our former way of life, but also there is the possibility of returning to it with renewed vigor and stubborn conviction. Renunciation of our thoughts about our former way of life is well worth every effort because its fruit is purity of heart. Once our thoughts are stilled and we have a mind "at peace," we wake up and experience God's presence.

The third renunciation is more difficult but we also need to let it happen if we are serious about the spiritual journey. Since thoughts come and go but we are not our thoughts, we must let go of our thoughts, including our thoughts of God who is known by unknowing. God is ineffable. We can know the face of Jesus through Scripture, but even there we must let Christ reveal himself to us without thought. We need to ask for the grace to detach ourselves from thoughts and let God be God for us. As difficult as this is, it is well worth the effort; in exchange for our fragile thoughts that come and go like clouds, we receive God who abides and unites us creatures with the whole of creation in a cosmic Christ consciousness.

Again this third renunciation requires us to let go of all thought of God. ". . . 'Come to the land which I shall show you'—that is, not to the one which you can know of yourself or find through your own effort, but to the one which I shall show you not only when you are unaware of it but even when you are not looking for it" (*Conf.* 3.10.6). This third renunciation is best arrived at by an un-thinking practice of contemplation. Language is tricky; it is not necessary in this renunciation. To prepare for passive recollection requires a contemplative practice of un-thinking, not of discourse. This passive recollection leads to the experience of illumination: "... such that once we have been led by his teaching and illumination we arrive at the perfection of the highest blessedness" (*Conf.* 3.10.6).

Our image of God is mediated through the senses. But through the practice of virtue, our hearts become purified and we are able to see God in a spiritual way, beyond our senses. In the fourth century there was already confusion about kataphatic prayer (with images) and apophatic prayer (without images). Abba Paphnutius says: "But the old man got so confused in his mind during the prayers, when he realized that the anthropomorphic image of the Godhead which he had always pictured to himself while praying had been banished from his heart, that he suddenly broke into the bitterest tears and heavy sobbing and, throwing himself to the ground with a loud groan, cried out: 'Woe is he, wretch that I am! They have taken my God from me, and I have no one to lay hold of, nor do I know whom I should adore or address'" (*Conf.* 10.3.4–5).

This painful moment along the spiritual journey is what I think John of the Cross is referring to when he describes the dark nights of the "senses" and of the "soul." He is not talking about the grief of loss that most seekers experience during the first two renunciations. We need images of God and ways of praying to lead us to pure prayer, to contemplation. But once we've met God "face to face," those images become obsolete or are totally transformed into a "new way of seeing." The spiritual senses take over. It's a time when

> ... every love, every desire, every effort, every undertaking, every thought of ours, everything that we live, that we speak, that we breathe, will be God, when that unity which the Father now has with the Son and which the Son has with the Father will be carried over into our understanding and our mind, so that, just as he loves us with a sincere and pure and indissoluble love, we too may be joined to him with a perpetual and inseparable love and so united with him that whatever we breathe, whatever we understand, whatever we speak may be God. In him we shall attain, I say, to that end of which we spoke before, which the Lord longed to be fulfilled in us when he prayed: "That all may

be one as we are one, I in them and you in me, that they themselves may also be made perfect in unity." And again: "Father, I
wish that those whom you have given might also be with me
where I am." (*Conf.* 10.7.2)

The fourth renunciation is seldom taught because most of us never
reach this stage in our spiritual journey, but if we know that the complete
journey will also require this renunciation, we want to be aware of it. This
renunciation requires us to renounce the thought of "self." The "I" in our
mind's eye must go. As in all organized descriptions about the phases of
the spiritual life, there may be some persons who experience these phases
differently or in a different order, perhaps bypassing some of them. St.
Thérèse of Lisieux, for instance, who was in her early twenties when she
was teaching her Little Way to her novices, probably was already in the
fourth renunciation.

This renunciation requires us to lay down our very self and merge with
Christ's own consciousness of the Father through the gift of the Holy
Spirit. Cassian talks about the completion and perfection of purity (*Conf.*
3.10.6), free of the thorns and thistles of sins (*Conf.* 3.10.5), even while we
are still in our body. Though walking in the flesh, one serves the Lord "not
according to the flesh" (*Conf.* 3.6.4). Self-love is replaced by love of God.
Self is reduced and renounced. Pure prayer springs up since all is God.
Equanimity is possible. A mind at peace is the fruit of renunciation.
Apostolic love abounds.

This fourth renunciation of "no self" might be what Buddhists speak of
as "emptiness." But we'd never know since there'd be no self to report it!
It seems to me to be the merging of the self not unlike the human nature
of Christ in the One Divine Person Jesus Christ, who is One in Trinity.

The four renunciations are means to an end and not an end in themselves. All ascetical practices should be modified in the light of the goal:
God. Each of these renunciations has its benefits: renouncing one's former
life gives one the space, time, and energy to start the spiritual journey;
renouncing one's thoughts purifies the heart and lets light in to help one
understand the God who is mediated through Scripture, or through
beauty and goodness in nature, or in one's very own experience.

Renouncing one's concepts of God brings one before God unmediated by texts and barriers that are only descriptive, not an actual experience of the presence of God. Finally, when the self is rooted out, all illusion, ignorance, and warring passions are tamed and all is God. Emptiness and dazzling darkness become the Transfiguration and (through the spiritual senses) a Transformation. No words can capture this participation in Christ.

When talking "about" anything, we are playing a trick on ourselves. We are pretending that "we know." But we only "know" from the outside. To use our garden image again, we are simply doing the work to make the flowers grow, but there isn't any way to know which flowers will grow and thrive. However, there is a sign that encourages us that we are following the tradition of those who have gone before us: that we have a "simple, one-pointed" consciousness. When we are aware of this kind of consciousness, we realize a joy and sense of inner freedom, much like a child.

These renunciations need not be dreaded. They are really the natural life cycle of birth to death. The requirements of each renunciation are what we call a vocation. We simply follow the call of grace no matter the obstacles. What is so welcoming about these teachings is that we are not alone. Others have gone before us and have worked in this garden of their souls. They've invented tools to do the work necessary at each of these four phases of renunciation.

2

AFFLICTIONS

Thoughts afflict the body through three doors: food, sex, and things. Thoughts afflict the mind through anger and dejection. And, finally, thoughts disease the soul through acedia, vainglory, and pride. In this chapter I will talk about how this happens and what the teachings from the desert tradition say about the afflictions that attack the body, the mind, and the soul.

Thoughts of the Body: Food, Sex, and Things

FOOD

The "food thought" in Christianity is governed by a light-hearted directive. Christ told his followers that what goes into the mouth is not as important as what comes out. Christianity has always had a bias toward service, love, and compassion. It contains directives for feasting and for being in communion with one another, suggesting rituals where food and drink are plentiful. No foods are ruled out. Later traditions of abstinence have been added, yet Christ himself ate and drank in a gracious manner according to the customs of his day. Reasons to be a vegetarian or to be ecologically sensitive to the food chain have expanded in our time, but Christians are not bound by laws that oppress the spirit of receiving all from God with graciousness. Nonetheless, food can be an affliction and an obstacle to our spiritual life.

The food thought is a good starting point to observe that we have thoughts. My body reminds me of my need for food in regular ways. When we honor those needs, the body responds with well-being, since for the spiritual life, we must be healthy. The austerities of the desert tradition are about training our bodies for endurance and stability, not about taming the beast inside. Since passions or afflictive thoughts can absorb us instead of serving us, our goal must be purity of heart, the state in which our thoughts are directed by our own will and then our mind is at peace. This is a realistic goal, but we must be aware that to be at peace we must know our thoughts with utmost honesty. In the darkness of ignorance, our thoughts will take over and snuff out our well-being.

> Thus entreating the dark shadows of our vices with the most pure eyes of our soul, we shall be able to expose them and to bring them into light, and we shall be in a position to disclose their causes and natures both to those who are free of them and to those who are still under their sway. In this way, according to the prophet, we shall pass through the first of the vices that burn our minds most terribly and immediately and be able to pass unharmed as well through the waters of the virtues that extinguish them, bedewed with spiritual remedies, we shall deserve, thanks to our purity of heart, to be led to a place of refreshment and perfection. (*Inst.* 5.3)

The thought of food is of benefit for the spiritual life. Because the body is so well tuned to give us signals about hunger and thirst, we can take those signals and use them as our first course of training. The first step in discriminating is to sort. The food thought goes like this: "I'm hungry. I would like a cup of tea. It would be nice to have a brownie with chocolate icing on it and maybe a small piece of fresh fruit. A sliced Bartlett pear would be nice." A bit later, "Yes, tea, a brownie, and fruit would make a great snack. Dinner is four hours away so the timing is good, too." Still later, "I want that tea I brought back from Ireland. I'll boil water in a real pot and make tea the right way with warm milk and real sugar. And maybe

I'll make enough for someone to join me. So maybe I'll want two cups of tea today at 4:00 p.m." So, the dialogue continues.

Notice: first there's the food thought, then the thought about the time to eat the food, then about the quality of the food and then about the quantity. Now the training, called fasting, is to check those four decisions: eating, the kind of food, when, and how much. So, fasting provides some helps about what foods I should eat for a snack, how expensive and available they are, when the appropriate time is, and how much I should eat or drink. Fasting is not always a negative thing. In reality, it's a middle way. It's just as objectionable to eat too little as to eat too much. Today may be a feast day so there's encouragement for me to eat something special and in a little more quantity, even to eat more frequently, perhaps taking an afternoon snack or an evening dessert before retiring.

There's one more thought about food that makes all the difference: motivation. Why is one eating or drinking? Gluttony is indiscriminate eating or drinking. Fasting is eating mindfully with full attention.

What does this have to do with the spiritual life? The food thought is the first in the series of eight thoughts. If I can notice and redirect my food thought and sustain right eating, then a rhythm in my life emerges that makes me fit for more difficult work. I am beginning to see how the mind works and how my thoughts rise and cluster into feelings and desires. We are not our thoughts or our hunger. We can eat or not eat. Actually the food thought diminishes when we don't entertain another thought about food. When we fast—which is balanced eating at designated times—our hunger has no major swings but is appropriately receptive and eager to enjoy a tasty meal. For the sensuous, fasting actually heightens appreciation. Overeating and indiscriminate eating diminish the sensibilities of the appetite and subtle distinctions of taste as well as the aesthetic beauty of food and drink.

A secondary, but helpful result of fasting in the spiritual life is the lesson that we cannot determine for another what is "good" for them. Both Cassian and Benedict emphasize personal discrimination. We are taught not to judge another. What is too much for one may not be enough for another; what is too much variety for one is needed by another's temperament. The training teaches us to use self-judgment and to restrain from judging anyone else. The role of the abbot is to hear the reasons for each monk's determination and to assist him in his personal sorting out of the best food management for him. Moderation is a good sign and extremes are to be suspected as having their roots in pride.

So food is the first thought but is essential for teaching how thoughts rise in the mind and how much "control" one really has in redirecting those thoughts to the right order of eating and drinking. If we do it well, the result is balance and a new strength in discrimination that can be used with other thoughts as well.

SEX

The thought of sex is the second thought and is a very persistent affliction of the body that seems to make even old men and women vigilant long past the body's ability to propagate.

Few reach the ideal of chastity, since the gift of equanimity about the thought of sex is rare. The truly chaste person has passed beyond all physical expressions of sexuality, beyond all erotic thoughts and even beyond subconscious desire. The chaste person experiences a joyous state of freedom, peace, and bliss.

Chastity is interior work of the heart. We must never judge another but do our own inner work. And we are always beginners. This affliction strikes anyone at anytime. The sex thought is like the food thought, only you desire another's body. The thought is more than physical, though the body is the home where this thought lives and takes up its residence. It lives beneath consciousness but seems to pulsate in every cell.

Since the sex thought is so pervasive, the desert tradition has a strong directive to be kind, compassionate, and understanding toward those who are conflicted with a sexual affliction. Judge not. There's the raw fact that when we judge another the sin enters us and soon we commit the same sin. It's a fact. How this works, I'm not sure, but that it does, I've seen in my own life.

The spiritual benefit of the transmuted thought of sex is enormous and should not be underestimated by simplistic negation. Chastity is a radical openness and receptivity to God. The contemplative's heart is not divided. It is pure.

The goal of a contemplative is to be naked, totally pure in heart before God. Cassian says that for a monk who has achieved this purity of heart even the night has become his delight (*Conf.* 12.8.6). When night arousals cease or are only from needs of nature, "[he] has without a doubt arrived at the state where he is the same at night as during the day; the same in reading as at prayer; the same alone as when surrounded by crowds of people; so that, finally, he never sees himself in secret as he would blush to be seen by men, and that inescapable eye does not see anything in him that he would wish to be hidden from human gaze" (*Conf.* 12.8.5).

He goes on to explain that, because sexual expression cools our energy, we must discern what kind of energy we want to store in our body. The three degrees of the sex thought can perhaps help us understand this. We are continent, celibate, or chaste. The first, continence, is resisting sexual activity. Here we are not inclined, we have no opportunity, or we are unable to perform the sex act. The second, celibacy, is governed by a particular vocation. A monk or nun renounces the use of sex. A married person renounces that use except with his or her designated and committed partner. The third, chastity, means renouncing even an inappropriate thought of sex. Chaste thinking is a practice, not simply the fruit of celibacy. "For as a person progresses in mildness and patience of heart, so also does he in purity of body; and the further he has driven away the passion of anger, the more tightly will he hold on to chastity. The body's seething heats will not lessen if one has not previously suppressed the mind's movements" (*Conf.* 12.6.1).

There are many occasions for self-deceit in regard to the sex thought, so we need to be honest with ourselves about the objects of our affections. Usually where there is a secret there is a lie, so it is good to have a wise elder with whom we lay out all our thoughts. This elder needs to know us well enough that we will want and welcome his or her direct and wise opinion. Being a monk or a nun or a married person doesn't prevent temptations to chastity. The teaching about it is seamless and logical. Sexual energies have a purpose in the spiritual life. These energies, when transmmuted, return to the body and heighten other energies that at once quicken the heart for ardor, zeal, and self-donation. They also stabilize the mind for study and clear thinking, and for right action and meditation.

To move our sexual energies toward ourselves, as in masturbation, or toward another outside of committed marriage is dividing the heart, dissipating human energies, and fragmenting the mind. As difficult as fidelity is, we have no other option if we seek equanimity or balance. Our motivation for celibacy and chastity is personal, and the benefits outweigh the frustration, since once we have a wholehearted commitment and have experienced a one-pointed mind, temptations lose a grip on us.

In teaching this over the years, I've noticed that sexual energies in our culture are so flat and overemphasized that it takes a good deal of stimulation to produce gratification. Conventional wisdom tells us to entertain sexual thoughts as much as possible in order to sustain and maintain sexual potency. The desert tradition recommends the opposite. Sexual instincts are so strong that all the monastic rigors can't fence them in. Sex thoughts simply are and are thick and passionate. The life energy, called sex, is the vehicle for enormous shifts in consciousness as well as for growth in commitment to one's vocation.

The disciple who has sublimated his or her sexual energy has all the benefits of sex and more. Cassian describes the fruit of celibacy:

> In all these instances, then, the more the mind has advanced to a more refined purity, the more sublimely it will see God, and it will grow in wonder within itself rather than find the ability to speak of it or a word to explain it. For just as the inexperienced person will be unable to grasp in his mind the power of this gladness, neither will the person who has experienced it be able to explain it in words. It is as if someone wished to describe in words the sweetness of honey to a person who had never tasted anything sweet. The one will in fact not grasp with his ears the agreeable flavor that he has never had in his mouth, while the other will be unable to give any indication in words of sweetness that his taste knows from its own enjoyment. Only by his personal knowledge of the atractive sweetness can he wonder silently within himself at the pleasant flavor that he has experienced. . . . [I]n the silence of his mind . . . [he] will cry out with the deepest emotion of his heart: "Wonderful are your works, and my soul knows them exceedingly." (*Conf.* 12.13.1–2)

He goes on to describe "that heavenly inpouring of spiritual gladness by which the downcast mind is uplifted by an inspired joy; over those fiery ecstasies of heart and the joyful consolations at once unspeakable and unheard of, by which those who occasionally fall into a listless torpor are raised as out of the deepest sleep to the most fervent prayer" (*Conf.* 12.12.6).

A heart that is not divided is at peace.

THINGS

Just as we are not our thoughts, we are not our things. Things are just another thought. If we give our hearts to things, we divert our attention from God. Things can be a substitute for God. If things take the place of God in our heart, then things become an idol. We worship things and give honor to things instead of to God. We have a right relationship with things when they mediate God, but things cannot be our goal.

Not only do things substitute for God, they also take on a life of their own. Things beget things: one thing, more things, better things; we must secure our things; we must have freedom to care for them, resources to protect them. The train of thoughts continues.

We can never be satisfied with things; there are never enough, never any stopping places. This causes restlessness, grasping.

Is there any way out of this? Yes, we must come to a profound awareness of our right relationship to things. It is an illusion that we possess anything. No possession(s) can satisfy our grasping tendency for more.

As an antidote, we must remember that all things come from God. We must remember that all things are gift to us creatures. The monastery is an alternative culture where the original order in the myth of the Garden of Eden is played out. The abbot, in the name of the community, bestows things, and the monk has all his needs met through the rituals and practices of obedience. The ancient investing ritual of a novice, wherein the monastic receives the habit, is an investing in new life. It is like receiving the new garment of baptism. Starting over, much like being born again, the novice gets a second chance. Entering a marriage or moving to a new city can also provide a similar occasion.

Obviously, renunciation differs for householders and monastics. A monastic renounces things in service of prayer and apostolic life. One symbol of this loss of control over things is to surrender one's discretion to give a gift. If a gift is given, it is given in the name of the community with the permission of the abbot. On the other hand, the householder secures and provides things and literally "goes through" the economy of work/profit/service for the sake of his or her home, family, and larger community. Both ways of life share in common a respect for things as gift and a return of things through service and labor.

Like all thoughts, the thing thought needs to be rooted out over and over again. It's an affliction that is susceptible to prevailing ways of "being in the world" today. To be in the world and not of it requires practices that counter the prevailing practices of consumerism and competition. The apostolic exhortations about working with one's hands, giving to the poor, sharing things in common, stewarding the earth, treasuring the manifestations of creation, if done even moderately, return a greater joy than the satisfaction of a single thing. All is gift!

We can never be complacent when it comes to things. The thing thought can return after years of humble living with only the things you need. Through lack of vigilance or heightened needs of old age or some period of insecurity, we begin to take back things. We start the cycle all over again.

A monastic can leave the monastery or a parent can leave the family to care for his or her things. God becomes this or that thing. Instead of not being able to live without God, he or she just can't live without this particular thing!

As monastic institutions go through their life cycle, evidence of things taking priority over the common life seems to be the clearest sign of a pending breakdown. It's a double sign since the need for things is less when the life of work and prayer is in balance. When the balance is off, there is more need for personal things to satisfy desires. When there are lots of things, there is little reverence. Prayer is replaced by thoughts of things. Works are done for self-gain and not for community or for God. Even if we are at prayer, our minds are shopping. We live on daydreams of more things, more travel, more relationships, and more entitlements.

Life is someplace else. Working at "getting things done" can have this same kind of dynamic.

Sorting needs to be a routine: not too much, not too little, not too high in quality, not too low in durability. Discrimination needs to replace greed and avarice. We must refrain from envying the things others have. Since all is gift and ownership is illusion, we rejoice if we need less and, once more, do not judge what another needs for his or her well-being and happiness.

Both householder and monastic must refrain from attachment to things. It is not optional for a Christian to ignore the poor. The three practices of fasting, almsgiving, and prayer might be translated: right use of things, giving and receiving according to need, and being grateful for all that is given. We can use things as a mirror. In each thing we can see and remember God rather than act or use things in themselves "as if" they were God. We can walk in the presence of God (not things) and tend to them graciously. When we do this, our life's work is more like ritual and worship. We are mindful and not full of worry or anxiety.

Thoughts of the Mind: Anger and Dejection

ANGER

God doesn't want us to be angry. The problem with being angry is that we can't pray when we are angry. We can't think and make good judgments when we are angry. Anger disqualifies us from spiritual work, say the elders of the desert. The good news is that anger can be entirely rooted out. The better news is that there are tools to do that that have been tested and found effective against the most stubborn, seemingly irreversible traumas. The best news is that anger passes quickly even if it rises again and again because of life's vicissitudes; however, we can learn to see it and resist its power. Eventually our response will be from our center of truth. Compassion for ourselves and the one who prompted our anger thought is possible.

The consequence of anger is inner blindness. Anger diminishes insights that spring from an honest gaze. When folks say they have a blind rage, it is literally true because blindness diminishes their spiritual capacity. Thinking an angry thought causes confusion. We perceive information poorly and then project it back in a distorted way. Those who meet us when we are exhibiting anger had better be on guard and should have no confidence in our words or actions. Anger disqualifies us from our own spiritual inner work and for spiritual counsel of another because we can not discern when we are filled with rage.

The description about anger continues, warning that unchecked anger may lead to depression (*Inst.* 9.4), and sometimes to madness or furious rage (*Inst.* 8.19.1–3). Because an angry person is contributing to universal disharmony, such madness may have consequences for the collective as well as for the individual.

Our fundamental goal is purity of heart. Thoughts are obstacles to that purity, that ability to see God. To "see God," we must still our thoughts. Anger quickens thoughts and casts them about. Anger fragments the mind. It is a subtle action against perceived threat. Hostile reactions are normal and natural, but not helpful in determining a reasoned solution to a given situation or issue.

According to Evagrius, prayer is lifting up one's mind to God: the expulsion of thoughts. Anger allows a free range to thoughts, casting them about wildly like horses resisting a roundup. In order to have a calm mind, therefore, you must root out anger.

Ability to discern spirits is the fruit of a clear mind, so we must not hold on to even a "little" anger. We must not rationalize that the size or seriousness of the injustice mitigates this teaching: when anger thoughts dominate our consciousness our soul is inaccessible.

In the face of injustice and oppression, the only option is a compassionate, non-violent response. Responses laced with anger only serve to promote and feed the cycle of violence. If strong measures that demand firm disciplinary action need to be taken, they should be done, but only when they arise from a pure heart and a clear head. Most of the time it is better to wait, assess the situation, and discern a proper, long-term response rather than react with quick rage. There is no teaching about righteous anger in the desert tradition.

Our own self-knowledge allows us to keep vigilance over our hearts. When we've done wrong or even if we perceive that others have felt wronged by us (though we may be innocent), we should reconcile with them before the setting of the sun. We ask for forgiveness because we are one body.

The teaching continues, asking us to root out the memory of wrong-doing; forget it as many times as it takes; face anger and stay in relationships. Friendships are divided by anger. Real friends want, and refuse, the same things. Equal in goodness, they renounce thoughts of anger. Both *lectio* and friendships strengthen the desire to meet God face to face.

"Hence, as we have said, only the ties of a friendship which is founded upon similarity of virtuousness are trustworthy and indissoluble, for 'the Lord makes those of one mind to dwell in the house.' Therefore love can abide unbroken only in those in whom there is one chosen orientation and one desire, one willing and one not willing. If you also wish to preserve this inviolable, you must first strive, after having expelled your vices, to put to death your own will and, with common earnestness and a common chosen orientation, to fulfill diligently what the prophet takes such great delight in: 'Behold, how good and how pleasant it is for brothers to dwell in unity.' This should be understood not in terms of place but spiritually. For it profits nothing if those who disagree about behavior and chosen orientation are together in one dwelling, nor is it a drawback to those who are of like vitue to be separated by distance. With God it is common behavior rather than a common location that joins brothers in a single dwelling, and fullness of peace can never be maintained where there is a difference of wills" (*Conf.* 16.3.4–5).

Frequent quarrels cool love; friends first part their hearts, then their shared time and place. This is no surprise since anger creates a road of adversarial thoughts, desires, and passions. If we feel that our anger will be solved "if only I lived alone without so and so," we find that this solution will not work. The anger will remain, and I only transfer it to things . . . knife, pen, and so forth (*Inst.* 8.19. 2–3).

Again this teaching is for those who have renounced their former way of life and are on the spiritual journey. Right effort is more than not being angry, it's staying mindful of God. We practice recollection and continually do *lectio divina* to put good thoughts in our mind. If our affliction of anger persists, we should seek out a wise elder, manifest our thoughts of anger, and ask for a way to break the cycle of these sticky thoughts. We should ask for help in sorting out our thoughts: have someone remind you that nothing is big enough, or serious enough, or urgent enough to "give-in" to the thought of anger. And even more than sorting our thoughts, we should seek out someone to assist us in refraining from acting in rage or even in an anger of low intensity.

Can thoughts of anger really be rooted out?

We have freedom to consent or not to consent to our thoughts, say the elders. Thoughts will come and thoughts will go. Consent is key. Thoughts can be redirected. But we must catch thoughts at the first inkling of awareness, like a snake's head, notice when it rises. The thought of anger feeds upon itself.

"The experience of days, months, and years without angry thoughts brightens the eyes, clears the skin, and quickens the walk of the seeker."[1]

"Absence of anger enlightens the mind. Without the thought of anger and other afflictive emotions we can read the books of experience, nature, and Scripture as manifestations of God. An ineffable joy replaces gloom, anxiety and calculating details of life that swing out of control."[2]

Our effort has to go beyond rooting out anger to reversing anger in order to imitate Christ. The role of sacrifice is to lay down one's life for another. To endure unjust persecution is the cost of discipleship.

"And what if the therapist to whom I paid a lot of money after my divorce said that I've got repressed anger and that I need to express it appropriately?" This question is very difficult because the teaching in the monastic tradition is very clear that the monk ought to be calm and that anger can and should be entirely rooted out. Good psychology and good spirituality ought to be cut from the same cloth so there should not be two opposing teachings about such a fundamental emotion as anger. But it seems to me that the two views on this matter clash. How do these views reconcile themselves with experience? Does expressing anger help or hinder one's meditation and apostolic love? We can find recommended actions about anger in many self-help books but seldom do we see such clear teachings from our Christian tradition, so I'll review them once again here:

1. Anger rises.
2. Anger can be noticed, faced, squared off with, confronted, and felt.
3. But anger need not be expressed as the object of a quarrel.
4. Expressing anger is practicing how to be angry.

5. Finding truth, expressing righteousness, seeking justice, and keeping peace are deliberate, discerned actions instead of consenting to anger.

6. Taking action on behalf of justice is compassion; we replace anger with right action. Anger can never be expressed toward another or toward ourselves to relieve the symptoms of this uncomfortable passion.

7. Right action can't be seen while one is blind with rage.

8. Anger agitates and creates a response of more anger and the cycle of violence continues.

9. Patience and long suffering is the opposite of repression.

10. Anger is a form of pride that indicates that I know the right action for another or that my dignity was insulted or that I'm to be the judge, jury, and executioner.

11. Humility would say that I don't know the right action without the grace of the Holy Spirit and that I have no dignity except in Christ Jesus. To imitate Christ's suffering is appropriate; anger is displaced by compassion. We understand and take action and seek no reward and are detached from both the good and the harm that might come to us.

12. Anger agitates the mind. Calm abiding and a contemplative gaze either at others, God, nature, or even myself is reduced in proportion to the anger.

13. We cannot pray when we are angry. No one can pray with us, either.

14. Anger makes us sick.[3]

15. To practice laying aside thoughts of anger is the opposite of repression. Patient waiting to respond in kindness at the appropriate moment is the opposite of reactive expression. To use lanuage crafted by Father Adrian van Kaam we could say that we aspire to "transpression," which is to notice the emotion, lift it up toward God in humble prayer for the guidance of taking action on behalf of others. Anger is a teacher that can lead us to purity of heart but only if we believe the good news that anger can be entirely rooted out, that with practice anger need not be expressed, nor repressed and that there are no residual effects that damage others or our psychological well-being.

To reduce or redirect anger we need tools. One such tool is guard of the heart that helps prevent occasions of anger. Another tool is manifestation of thoughts to a wise elder. This kind of confessing requires laying out our thoughts of anger for the purpose of letting them be unaccompanied by another thought and reducing attachment to them. These tools will be discussed in detail in further chapters of this book.

DEJECTION

Another affliction of the mind is dejection. Dejected thoughts lead to the passion or state of depression. Not all depression is a result of anger, but it's good to sort out the causes of depression because the way in to depression sometimes is a clue to the way out.

Sometimes, indeed, depression is caused by unresolved anger. Anger sinks deeper and deeper into psychic levels not available to our conscious choice and subtle directives. Another cause of depression is grief, a residue from the loss of something that was held dear. Perhaps it was a person, a thing, our bodily well-being, or some change that happened to us and not of our choice. A third cause for depression is the desire for a gain that has not been realized. This is another form of grief. It causes us to mourn the loss of a dream, an opportunity not had, a closure irrevocably cut off, or an option not chosen that was, perhaps in hindsight, even a bad decision. A toxic environment causes some depressions. And there is also depression that has no apparent reason—it comes out of nowhere. One type is chemical. Another type of depression that seems to have no apparent reason is existential dread. That kind of dejected thoughts is less differentiated but seems to be a dark mood that challenges well-being. It's the desire "not to be" that sometimes is in conflict with our nature "to be" in existence. This dread just is and can be noticed and sourced in our freedom and autonomy of choice for life. And finally there's depression that come from sin. In this case it is clearly caused by our own choices. Depression ruminates about stored-up injuries or memories of hurt. Feelings such as resentment, regret, and cynicism become an abiding preoccupation. Or sometimes there's no thought, just a bad mood—the mind is unavailable for thinking and even feeling when depression is darkest.

The cause of depression must be taken into consideration. If it is anger, forgiveness helps. If it is grief, then we must begin the long process of letting go. If it is chemical, medication can perhaps remedy it. If it is the environment, a change might relieve the underlying cause. If it is sin, confession, absolution, and making amends can work wonders. Some depression is a symptom of addiction, or it may be many-faceted.

When you are in full-blown depression, there are admonitions from the elders: stay in relationships, because isolation is harmful when dejected thoughts assault us. Refrain from all thoughts that put us down, especially thoughts of doing harm, such as suicide. Self-denigration is actually a perverse form of pride. We are dejected because we are not receiving from others and from ourselves the praise and exaltation we "deserve" or expect.

The training about how to get out of dejection is to notice a sad thought and say, "It just is." "I feel sad." Then count on God's grace. Redirect out of your consciousness all such depressive thoughts even if they are based in reality. Depressive thoughts are not helpful. Truth usually comes in even, neutral, and simple thoughts that "just are," no more, no less. One practice of the saints is to "think" truth or not to think at all. Simply participate in ceaseless prayer, they say. But this gets ahead of our story.

For now, when dejected thoughts come, check them early, dispatch them, dash them on the rock, which is Christ.

If our depression is from sin, then we need to make a confession and ask for absolution. Sometimes in dejection, our sins don't allow us a normal desire for contrition and reconciliation. In this case we can confess the "desire for the desire" of a feeling of genuine contrition, reconciliation, and the grace to make amends.

The sacrament of penance has enormous benefits for all Christians. We need not be Catholic to participate in this amazing, hallowed ritual. The abiding, low-intensity type of depression lifts as we amend our faults and correct our ways of thinking, talking, and acting. We must resist the morbid suffering of not caring. This calls for a strong practice of faith because we have no inclination or incentive from our feelings. We must strive against acting out the way we feel. Our self-centered preoccupation needs to be replaced with patience, with self-donation.

If our environment is too heavy for our mood to manage, we might need, for a time or for a lifetime, to move out of situations that are too toxic. It's simple humility to admit that environmental pressures are too intense of an influence to be able to "hold my own." Usually one needs to seek the wisdom of a wise elder about this to assure ourselves that we are not just running away from obligations and commitments that are just now deep enough to work toward our salvation through purifying them. But there are times when the prudent thing is to move on (Luke 10:10).

As to thoughts of suicide, there's always an alternative: forgiveness (always a way out). Sometimes in this case the dejected one can't "feel" that any other option would bring relief. Helpers must gently and consistently insist that suicide is not an option that will relieve suffering. In fact, it will only compound it. But if we take one step at a time, the depression will pass.

There is a benefit to dejection. It leads to compunction and it fires up our desire for God. Because dejection replaces the fruits of the Spirit with negativity, a despondent and fragmented mind cannot be at peace. But when this dejection thought begins to be dissipated, peace of mind is restored. We experience a mystery with no conceptual definition where undifferentiated energy and formless data tell us this is "the way it is." A sincere grief for wrongdoing begins to soften our hardness of heart. This movement within us prevents acedia.

Soon we'll experience sorrow again, but this time it will be the sorrow of compunction, a wholesome sorrow. Dejection cycles round and round about the harm done to me. Compunction has a reverential feeling. Compunction helps us see that we need mercy, but it also tells us we are much more loved than we ever deserved. The shift from depression to compunction is difficult. Since dejection resides in the subconscious, when we are dejected we need compassionate care. It is difficult for us to shift into an abiding disposition of *penthos* (compunction) even after conversion of heart. We need grace.

In summary, detachment, not indifference, is the preferred thought. When we are dejected we must let go of any part of our lifestyle that is sinful. And even if our depression is from a chemical unbalance, we can practice faith.

The fruit of dejection is to be aware, moment by moment, of the true nature of reality. Depression weans us from our physical senses and awakens our spiritual senses. We begin the third renunciation practice: seeing without images in an undifferentiated reality. We experience the dark abyss of nothingness. We are emptied of all that is illusion. When darkness lifts we see the beauty in the smallest trifle, even the dazzling darkness of emptiness.

Thoughts of the Soul: Acedia, Vainglory, and Pride

ACEDIA

My ability to discern sleeps and is turned off. I'm separated from reason and awareness (*Inst.* 10.4).

Acedia is difficult to detect. My mind is sluggish. My thoughts are slow and diminished. If I have any feelings at all, I feel moody. I have distaste for spiritual things. Scripture and spiritual reading are repulsive. I no longer enjoy going to Mass or saying any prayers. I want my time back from obligations. My ability to notice thoughts is gone and is replaced by a bad mood.

What is so serious about acedia is that, as dejection leads to suicide, acedia leads to soul-death. I feel like rejecting any further time or energy on the spiritual journey. I've had it! No more spiritual-life seeking for me!

Notice that I'm the same person who renounced my former way of life. I renounced thoughts of food, sex, things, anger, and dejection. I diligently did all the practices of fasting, vigils, discernment, and prayers. Now I've simply stopped. The noonday devil has overtaken my zeal and replaced it with a dead heart (Ps. 91:6).

What is acedia? It is an affliction of motivation, of intention, of reasons for doing spiritual work. It usually afflicts a practitioner when there is no return, no satisfaction, or consolation from spiritual works. It is very serious because it makes me vulnerable to making decisions I might regret later: to leave, start my own monastery, become a priest or prioress, or transfer to another community or another job.

While my soul is asleep, I am weary of doing anything good or bad. The tragedy that can happen is that I can die without having really lived.

These are the signs of acedia:

I dislike the place and am repulsed by the members of my community. These feelings can evolve into contempt, public disdain, and fault finding.

I take leave often and visit folks away from the monastery or bury myself in work.

Occasionally I sleep all day, missing early prayer. Coming late most of the time becomes a pattern.

I stop spiritual work—common prayer, prayers in my cell. Ceaseless prayer is simply too much effort. I can't stay anywhere for very long. I feel restless and have no time for *lectio*.

I begin to feel that this place is actually a barrier to my spiritual practice. I begin to fantasize about a distant "perfect" monastery. The thought of leaving becomes almost a heroic virtue, rather than simply an option. I try to talk others into leaving with me. "This place will never change," I say to them. I have a restless mind and cause restlessness in others.

If I leave in a state of acedia, my new work will be external only, since I will not bring any interior practices to my new venture. If I stay here I will do nothing.

Even though my choice is tempered with anger, depression, and little awareness during this time that my soul is asleep, I have no capacity for contemplation, no insight for my work, no wisdom for others. I have made a choice away from sanctification, and if I die in this state I may be making a choice away from my salvation.

Cassian's teaching in his *Conferences* says that we can move through acedia. We can rededicate ourselves to spiritual work because our spiritual work is just now at a place of transforming power. Just as we started with the training of fasting, guard of our heart, manifesting our heart to a wise elder, sorting our thoughts, keeping vigils, observing the common life, we must now begin all these practices again as if we were a novice. The other major help out of the grasp of acedia is that we return to physical work and accept the discipline of manual labor.

The teaching goes on to say that, in order to reverse tendencies that come from the thought of acedia, we must do the opposite of what we feel. If we feel like roaming, we must stay in our cell. If we feel like wasting time, we must avoid idleness and laziness. If we feel like traveling and going for a visit to a distant relative, we must stay home and stick to our routine. In that routine we work mindfully, we eat and drink moderately, we do the work assigned to us without grumbling. We check off our list of occupations that give us permission to skip community obligations and the routine of personal practices.

In dejection we are told to stay at common table and to be engaged with others. In acedia we need to avoid others who have the same affliction. Sometimes it isn't folks who are dissatisfied that are harmful to us, but simply those who like to chatter and move away from the serious keeping of interior guard of the heart. It doesn't take much to allure us away from our call to silence.

When we work honestly for those who are in need, it offsets our desires for someone else's possessions. We need to resist people who give us gifts because those gifts feed an autonomous lifestyle that fosters detachment from the economic commitment of marriage or the monastery.

There is a teaching about leisure when you are under the affliction of acedia. Refrain from taking too much time "for myself" because, instead of receiving energy, idle time can easily kill our industriousness, perpetuating spiritual sloth—-therefore, study and be quiet (*Inst.* 10.7.3–5).

Like the previous afflictions, there are benefits to this purifying suffering, to the affliction of acedia. Our intentions are tested, and if we labor and practice, "in faith" rather than "in consolation," we notice our motivations and can check which things we do only for our own self-interest and reverse those tendencies.

Another benefit to acedia is what happens to us when we counter acedia with manual labor. We see the beauty and health of "work" as a spiritual practice. When we do manual labor accompanied with the interior practice of ceaseless prayer, our minds return to simple devotion to God. When self-chatter stops even for a moment, we come to a peace of mind equal to that contemplative cup of coffee on the back porch. Eventually our work is our prayer and our prayer is our work. They become interchangeable. We shift from getting things done to simply doing things in the moment. Our attention becomes sharp and we do things well, not simply for ourselves but because in the doing we find harmony in the universe as a co-creator. We experience the sacredness of the moment.

With the practice of manual labor comes a depth of silence. We begin to have a preference for quiet. To refrain from speaking even about good things trains one to listen, to rest, to receive, to observe, and to be present to the moment. When the mind is at rest, acedia modulates and we begin again to develop a fervent heart. Our mood swings moderate and our body feels the rhythm of alternation between rest and work.

Not only does my mood become more settled, but a new feeling emerges, called compunction. It's a gift, a right feeling before God. It is the virtue of one who is "pricked to the heart," who has become conscious of his or her distance from God and now has an altered awareness and ardor for God, her heart's desire.

Compunction softens the soul dried up by dejection and acedia. We begin to feel sorrow, tenderness, and joy springing from sincere repentance. Sometimes it's a burning state, like being in love, not like a reaction to an incident. Compunction resolves acedia through a heightened relationship with God. Compunction has no moods or periods of doubt. Like a sinner in constant need of God's mercy, it is intimate and close to mystery. We feel purified and naked before God, without shame or guilt. Pierced to the heart, it is our relationship with God that matters.

The good news of compunction is that it prevents the next two afflictions of the soul. If we don't get over anger or dejection, our symptoms pass but leave us ripe for the next affliction. Anger and dejection ripen into acedia. If acedia blooms without being healed, what flowers is a full-blown spiritual disease of the soul called vainglory and pride.

Vainglory

Vainglory is an affliction of the soul that makes me do all the right things for the wrong reason. Vainglory is taking credit for good actions. The true meaning of glory is God's presence, and vainglory takes that presence to mean "self" rather than God. This is an affliction of motivation. We shift all our attention toward the self. Vainglory causes me to be so conscious of what others think of me, of how I am perceived, that I actually perceive myself through what I think others think of me. I'm in major delusion.

Spiritual directors may have difficulty detecting this affliction because this form of pride prevents me from presenting myself truthfully and therefore often communicating this self-deception not only to myself but also to my spiritual director. We dupe others and ourselves, then others give us feedback that isn't based on reality. The deception abounds.

The layers upon layers of vainglory multiply. Often one who is filled with vainglory tends to become a leader, a spiritual professional, or a public person. When the vainglory thought makes me so conscious of what others think, I will change to meet those expectations, hoping they will like me more and more as I mirror the crowd's pleasure and feed their image of me.

The teaching about vainglory is that puffing myself up in vainglory is a partner to dejection, which is putting myself down. Both vainglory and dejection are forms of pride, of not recognizing the truth as it is.

Vainglory is presumption when I act based on overconfidence. We replace God with self as the object of worship. If glory is the experience of the presence of God, then we cannot take glory to ourselves. That is empty, an illusion; it is vain. Shame is the inverse of glory, a terrible knowledge, that awful nakedness we feel without the garment of light. We need not dwell in shame when we are redeemed, but in adoration and reverence.

The affliction of vainglory attacks spiritual seekers. It's a wound of the spiritually proficient. It happens to those of us who have mastered the earlier afflictions of food, sex, things, anger, and so on. I twist the truth in order to move toward self instead of toward God. If a stilled heart is full of self, then my spiritual powers of keen insight and single-minded concentration may look good but be brutally devastating. I appropriate to myself what belongs to God. I look good: dress, voice, vigils, fasts, prayers, reading, practices, obedience, silence, and outward humility. Or even if I am bad, no one is as bad as I am. To be the worst sinner is to glory in one's wicked ways, more than anyone else in need of God's mercy does. Either excess, good or bad, when attributed to the self is vainglory and puffs up the ego.

Vainglory is subtle. It is an affliction that makes vices out of virtues. Even my moderation is better than anyone else's moderation. I'll not pray in front of others since they will think me holy. So, then I don't pray at all. Practices (fasting, vigils, and manifestation of thoughts) might become vices so I'll not do them. Vainglory winds through all the virtues, say the elders. It can penetrate all the gains of previous renunciations.

Just as anger disqualifies me from the work of giving wise counsel to another, so vainglory disqualifies me from ministry. A public role that is dressed in spiritual language masks the deception of vainglory—manipulating others under our own care instead of helping them toward God. This is the opposite direction of ministry.

To detect if we are ready and ripe for ministry, we should discern with a seasoned elder. As we share our practices, this elder should probe our motivations.

There's no easy way out of vainglory because, when we begin to feel confident and proud of passing out of the affliction of vainglory, we become proud of that fact and this self-satisfaction is worse than the first affliction. So, we should refrain from any belief that we have evolved past the spiritual practices and don't need fasting, prayers, guard of the heart, and watchfulness over our thoughts. If we are beyond them, an outside authority must confirm that because from the inside we will not know. In the meantime, rather than rushing into public ministry, we should humbly await a call to it because such a ministry would encourage the "external viewing of myself from the point of view of others." Hence the encouragement of feedback that we may take to self and not to God.

The most telling indication that we are in the grip of vainglory is revealed in daydreams, excessive imagining of situations where we are the center of attention. Through the practice of watchfulness, we need to stay in the present moment, noticing subtle signs of boasting, of being competitive, of telling remarkable tales about ourselves, of seeking and taking credit, of playing the role of the hero.

We must continually edit, redirect, and change thoughts about ourselves that are either high (praise) or low (dejection). The practice of humility is to think about myself exactly as I am. Vainglory intoxicates the mind (*Inst.* 11.15).

Any thought of envy is also a thought of vainglory. (It is often a result of dejection when we see the well-being of another.) We take to ourselves glory that properly belongs to God through another. Envy can propel the soul sidewise distorting our gratitude for given gifts.

Like the previous afflictions, however, there are many benefits from purifying and overcoming vainglory.

We can better discern our motivation for apostolic service. We also overcome embarrassment and ambivalence about our motives since a response that is neither high nor low but humbly based on truth gives me interior poise.

When we are poised, we can either work in ministry in the monastery or at home because the inner work is the same: we must watch our thoughts. Whether we are alone or with others, whether we live in a cloister or are on the road with a tour bus, doesn't matter. "So while a solitary life is helpful to know my thoughts, the practice of watchfulness can be a mental substitute for the desert culture of a monk or a hermit."[4]

Our confidence is placed securely in God. We need not try to cultivate specific virtues. We simply lay aside thoughts and give God glory (ceaseless prayer) and God raises up the virtues necessary for our situation. We are safeguarded by the abiding disposition of compunction. If we give God glory and ask for mercy for ourselves, then a Christ consciousness emerges.

When the "I-thought" begins to dominate again that is a sign to "watch and pray."

PRIDE

"Doing the wrong things for the wrong reasons" is the affliction of pride. It is end-stage disease of the soul.

There are two kinds of pride: spiritual and carnal. Spiritual pride, the sin of the proficient, is turned toward God. My inner being becomes my reference point, and I act "as if" God did not exist. A radical defiance spawns audacious thoughts against God, even a hatred of God. A proud person has powers, even spiritual ones, and uses them confidently in "my own name" and "for my own benefit." If I have spiritual pride, I use my power to condemn or to hurt others if they get in the way.

"God can be damned for all I care," I say to myself. Hell doesn't exist and if it did, I would not want to be on the side of a God that creates hell. End-stage defiance is what we see here. I am the same person who renounced my former way of life and all the thoughts of my former way of life. I have all the powers I have honed through doing the practices and training my mind. But now I know what is good for all. No discernment is necessary since my thoughts are God.

This kind of spiritual pride leaves us open to demonic forces because we renounced the world and took refuge in Christ, then renounced our former way of life both exteriorly and interiorly, then took it all back slowly or in a moment of weakness. Now we are skilled and trained in spiritual feats of concentration. We renounce the way of life called renunciation. Then we become full of pride. We can determine the good and the way we want to accomplish it. We now renounce God. This is the sin of blasphemy.

The teaching of the desert tradition goes on to say that where once there was prayer without ceasing, and mindfulness of the presence of God, now there is only self-adoration. This is spiritual pride in full bloom.

Another lesser form of pride is carnal pride. Here we don't deny God or go against God so much as we just make choices for our self instead of God. This pride endows me with thoughts of exaggerated self-importance. It is common to everyone subject to self-willed defiance. "I need this more than someone else." "I'm worth it." "I'm a unique person. . . ." My reference is my own thoughts, desires, and passions, not God. I don't intend harm or feel inclined toward evil, I simply live for myself.

Is this teaching saying that it's either God or our personal tastes, likes, and self-expression? No, God makes us, for God and in God, so there's no Abrahamic choice to kill Isaac in this teaching. The point is to choose God and then in, from, with, and through God do what is best for the self and others. God comes first by way of order of importance and total claim on our attention and adoration. We are called to sacrifice for the good of another. We donate the self. It's the way of faith rather than the way of the world. Remember this is the stuff of the interior journey. There is an awareness and choices to be made since there's consciousness of intentions and a range of choices for doing the loving thing. There's a presence of God that is part of the experience of being "me." So, it's in this light that carnal pride is taking the self-road rather than the journey with Christ.

Each thought gets distorted. I don't share food. I lust for another's affection or things. I seduce someone for my own pleasure. I grasp things without consideration of how much is enough or what other people might need. I feel my anger is justified. I am above others and put others down. I devote time to myself instead of to my spiritual practices. The training of my thoughts collapses and I return to myself. God's word isn't defied as much as it is forgotten and dismissed as "not for me."

Carnal pride is different from spiritual pride because the self takes precedence over God, whereas spiritual pride actually places the self "as God."

How can carnal pride be detected? It starts with a lukewarm spiritual fervor. I have renounced my former way of life, but then ever so slowly I reclaim old patterns. I return to my earlier ways. My outside demeanor is rough, not gentle and kindly. I feel superior to others. I know I need not deny myself any needs. After all, I determine what is good for me. Formerly I had clear eyes and radiant skin. Now my eyes are dead. My heart is cold, my affect is flat, and socially I'm bored. Restraint is not even an option, since now I believe that in my earlier life it was a mistake to be so stupid. Now, I believe, it is time to take care of myself. No outside authority can determine what is good for me. If they get in my way, they are going to regret it, especially if they ever need anything from me. I am not a pushover.

Often one can observe that with carnal pride comes a look that clearly indicates the affliction. A person caught in carnal pride has an outward gait that is a strut, a loud voice that dominates conversations, a noisy and excessive mirth that is ostentatious. If this person is silent, it is a bitter silence, an unreasonably gloomy mood. This person speaks with authority, answers with rancor, and says whatever is on his or her mind. She feels free to insult others but feels that no one should mess with her (*Inst.* 12.27.5). Traditional times are over, she says, and so is traditional wisdom.

How can this affliction of pride be rooted out? We know God's mercy like a "good thief" can prevail even at our last breath. No one is ever lost. In fact, there's good reason to posit universal salvation.

Most persons afflicted with pride don't want to be rid of it because it feels so good to be so right. Part of the end stage of pride is a feeling of being sacrosanct: no need of repentance, conversion, or change of heart.

Often there is an event that changes our minds. The pride-filled life usually doesn't work. In crisis there is a change of heart that softens our self-confidence allowing God to rise up again with a welcoming invitation. What can we do? I've been heading in the wrong direction.

We need to start all over on the spiritual life as a novice. We need help to sort out our thoughts. We'd be most fortunate to find a good teacher who has mastered the eight thoughts. We should not simply rely on gray hairs but notice if this teacher has afflictions that are not yet resolved. If we cannot find a wise elder, the next best thing is to sort out things in our own cell. We should start by looking at our thoughts, then take action to be in right relationships. Confess our sins. Receive absolution. Make amends.

We can see, in the light of the affliction of pride, that we need to stay with spiritual training early, often, and always. The tools for spiritual practices are described in the writings of the elders, but they are rarely taught now. It is simply assumed that the monastic way of life teaches the seeker how do use the tools.

The rest of this book is about those tools and how to use them. But we must be sure we understand that tools are just that: they are tools. They can help us live in God's presence. They can help us know God. But they are not revealed by God in Scripture. We can learn about them only from those who have gone before us. But it is we who must pick up these tools and use them for ourselves. Do these tools quicken our step, warm our heart, and lighten our minds? If the answer is yes, then our garden work is successful.

Are there tools that are specific for each affliction? Yes, fasting is an antidote for food; checking dreams and manifestation of thoughts to an elder is an antidote for sex thoughts; staying in our cell helps us put things in order; watching our thoughts and guarding our heart prevents anger from entering our innermost center; vigils can offset depression; manual labor moves out acedia. You get the picture.

However, there is much crossover in the practices, so it is easier to present them in three groups: negative tools, positive tools, and social tools. Each set can then be seen as a set of tools for a particular garden. Most of the time, we don't need all of them. If we use any one of them with care we often find that all the work that needs to be done is finished. So, we enjoy all the tools but use the one or ones that fit the needs of what's in season in our garden.

3

NEGATIVE TOOLS

If we want to root out negative thoughts that drag us down and away from loving others and God, we need to find a way to get thoughts from controlling our mind. In a sense these thoughts have to be backed out and not allowed to settle in, so that we do not act as if we were our thoughts. Some tools are specifically used to "un-think" while other tools are used "to think" thoughts that replace the afflictive thoughts. This chapter addresses the un-thinking, or negative process, of the thinking mind. Again, the reader needs to see the mind as *nous* in the Greek concept. It's the locus of the person wherein the individual has control. We take initiative, we intuit wisdom, we discern right action, we feel the loving desire for God and the good of others more than our own self-interest. The mind is the noble residence of the person's identity and entity. Only I can see with my eyes and experience behind my eyes the solidity of truth. Only I can enter the invisible world of my mind and be in dialogue with the many voices of choice and be warmed by the laughter of another. If we would but un-think, there'd be space enough to dwell in the conversation we call Trinity. But this is the contemplative experience ahead of our story here.

There are many other tools to accomplish this reprogramming of our inner consciousness but for our purpose in this book we are examining only the ones that have left a trail for us to follow in our Christian tradition:[1]

1. guard of the heart
2. watchfulness of thoughts
3. fasting
4. dreams
5. ceaseless repentance

GUARD OF THE HEART

Guard of the heart is a physically demanding practice. When we guard our hearts, we prevent obstacles to prayer from entering our consciousness by placing our primary effort and attention at the entrance of our heart. We focus on how we feel. We develop ways to sense when we "don't feel at peace" in our heart. We notice what kinds of people, places, and things endanger this well-being. In other words, we protect our heart by what we call guard of the heart. This effort requires resisting encounters with people, places, and things that, after the experience, will linger "on one's heart."

A word about heart and mind. In the early tradition the word "mind" (*nous*) meant heart and head. It seems that philosophers, reflecting Greek ways of thinking, used the word "mind" to express the theory of contemplation. "Heart" is more of a biblical word.[2] It was much later in Scholasticism and indeed in our own psychological age that we speak of the split between the heart and the head, the heart-brain, and other ways of unifying our experience of our very person. For the sake of tools, I've just used heart as the bigger experience, and thought in the mind as the detailed data-experience whether it comes from the head center, the heart center, or the gut center. To name the impulse from the gut is still a "thought" registering in the mind. This is an endless debate and I've cautioned myself over and over again simply to teach this as clearly as I understand it.

When seekers would go to a desert elder, they attended to the movements of the heart (of the mind), suggestions, inner promptings. When such an impulse or inner prompting develops into an outward deed, into consent of the will, it would be too late to show all this to the director. One must then go to a confessor and resolve not to wait till next time. Elders "differentiated between moments of temptation. There is the *prosbolē* (suggestion in thought), which is free from blame (*anaitios*). . . . Next follows the *syndias-mos* (coupling), an inner dialogue with the suggestion (temptation), then *palē* or struggle against it, which may end with victory or with consent (*synkatathesis*), actual sin. When repeated, such acts produce a *pathos* (passion), properly speaking, and, in the end, a terrible *aichmalōsia*, a 'captivity of the soul,' which is no longer able to shake the yoke of the Evil One.

"The proper object of *exagoreusis tōn logismōn* (revelation of thoughts) is the first stage of this process, the *prosbolē*. One must crush the serpent's head as soon as it appears. . . . All this is done through an entire strategy: *nepsis* (vigilance), watchfulness, the guarding of the heart (*custodia cordis*) and of the mind, prayer, especially the invocation of the name of Jesus, and so forth."[3]

When we guard our heart, we refrain from being in contact with energies that will interfere with our effort to pray ceaselessly and eventually with our experience of God's presence. We cannot engage in ceaseless prayer and simultaneously engage in afflictive thoughts and emotions. So, guard of the heart prevents easy entry of any disturbance into our heart. It requires us to take control of what goes in and what the heart has to "feel."

Guard of the heart is a practice that is most helpful once we've made a resolution about something. When we want strongly to follow through with our resolution we should guard our heart from doubt and from counter experiences that move us away from our resolve. The fruit of guard of the heart is a heart full of strength and commitment to our vocation, our work, and our relationships. Since the heart provides us our innermost experience of "being with" God, we should guard all our choices to "be with" God.

An example of guarding our heart is to notice when we feel anger rising. Is there a pattern? Is it when we're with certain company? Does it follow after watching hours of football and drinking beer? Is it after we've watched certain TV programs? Once we find a pattern, when we're trying to decide how to invest our time and energies, we then can guard our hearts from those factors harmful to our calm mind and our prayer. When thoughts rise that incline us to anger, then we practice guard of the heart and foreclose those activities. Guard of the heart is preventative and helps us anticipate rather than be a victim. Actions and their results on our hearts should be no mystery. Our hearts are sensitive to everything we do. The people we are with change us for the better or for the worse. Our environment is an energy field that either supports our way of life or challenges it. Guard of the heart is taking care of our heart and protecting it for our heart's desire.

WATCHFULNESS OF THOUGHTS

Watchfulness of thoughts is the practice of catching a thought, perception, or feeling at its first inkling, in its initial reflexive moment. When we watch our thoughts, we anticipate and are on the alert for thoughts that seem to enter our consciousness and may become afflictions, such as sex or anger. Watchfulness of thoughts is a practice of simple awareness, noticing and letting thoughts come "as they are" without resistance or editing. Then we simply let them go. Letting go is actually not the way it happens. A thought will go away by itself if we don't accompany that thought with another thought. To let go of a thought is simply to refrain from the next thought. So some folks prefer the language of "letting be" instead of "letting go."

Watchfulness of thoughts helps us remember that all thoughts are only thoughts: "I am not my thoughts, feelings, or passions. I have thoughts, but I am not my thoughts." Watchfulness of thoughts is training in *logismos*, seeing the sequence and circular nature of thoughts. As we get more proficient we can detect at what point we consent to the thought. When we do that, we couple that thought with the next thought and give it life.

When we watch our thoughts, we make consent to them an act of consciousness and bring the full strength of our will to that consent, rather than the sometimes half-awareness we experience in the realm of habit. This reduces unconscious mindlessness from being in control.

John Climacus in his famous *The Ladder of Divine Ascent* reports the distinctions hallowed before his time (579–649 C.E.). He writes:

> Among the discerning Fathers, distinctions are recognized between provocation, coupling, assent, captivity, struggle and the disease called passion, which is in the soul. These blessed Fathers say that provocation is a simple word or image encountered for the first time,

which has entered into the heart. Coupling is conversation with what has been encountered, whether this be passionately or otherwise. Assent is the delighted yielding of the soul to what it has encountered. Captivity is a forcible and unwilling abduction of the heart, a permanent lingering with what we have encountered and which totally undermines the necessary order of our souls. By struggle they mean force equal to that which is leading the attack, and this force wins or loses according to the desires of the spirit. Passion, in their view, is properly something that lies hidden for a long time in the soul and by its very presence it takes on the character of a habit, until the soul of its own accord clings to it with affection.[4]

So, it's easier to cut off the thought at its earliest stage rather than when it's in the later stage ready to take up residence in habit and previous conditioning. To catch our thoughts we must be watching and aware.

We can practice watchfulness of thoughts at any time. Some formalize this vigilance and watchfulness through meditation techniques or through journaling. Watchfulness of thoughts is a first step; a further step is to manifest our thoughts to a wise elder. We'll discuss this later, but to manifest a thought to an elder effectively stops the looping around of thoughts that are spinning into emotions and cyclic patterns of compulsions.

An example of watching thoughts might be to take a moment before cooking dinner, or getting ready to do the dishes. Thoughts rise. Look at them. Observe them.

"I'm tired. Some one else should do the dishes. I did the cooking. There's no appreciation for what I do around here. I'm just a worker." "I need more money for a new car. There's already a leak in the trunk that I must get fixed. Don't have any time till Saturday." Notice the thoughts as they rise. If I think about them and consent to them, I'll think about another thought that goes down that same path. Good thoughts seem to enliven me, but depreciative thoughts circle around: more thoughts of anger, depression arises and my thoughts then take on a life of their own.

So, given the above sequence, in order to watch my thoughts I would first notice the initial one: "I'm tired." If the next one rises, "Some one else should do the dishes," I'd check that one so that the sequence doesn't go down a dark trail. The practice of watching thoughts is the first step in giving me more control over my thoughts. I don't have to consent to any of the thoughts. Even the thought "I'm tired" is just a thought. I can simply watch it. The alternative is to get hooked on it and feel more tired than I did before I was aware of the thought. Noticing is enough to free us from the tyranny of thoughts.

Watchfulness of thoughts is the first step in liberation from the cycle and tyranny of thoughts that afflict the body, the mind, or the soul. By watching we gain distance from those thoughts, and from that distance we sense our ability to accept that thought, to reject it, or to simply let it be. It has no power over me. This distance eventually becomes poise, the opposite of compulsion. Watchfulness of thoughts works toward commitment also, since it makes me more ready for thoughts that fit my choices, and more able to notice thoughts that move me away from my resolve. I learn to let it be and am not surprised at what thought rises in my mind. It's just a thought. The fruit of watchfulness of thoughts is leisure in its literal sense to "let be."

There are two other recommended practices to deal with thoughts that are in the "thinking" or positive category: ceaseless prayer is one and the other is a counter-thought (*antirrhesis*) which you think instead of the one rising. We cannot think two thoughts at the same time.

FASTING

Food is a way of getting to know your thoughts. We all experience hunger and we can all tune into our thoughts, feelings, and passions about food. If we can re-direct our thoughts about food and about drink then we are "in training" for controlling other thoughts like sex, things, anger, and the like. Fasting—the middle way—means to eat at designated times, to eat enough but not too much, and to eat what's given.

Abstinence refers to fasting from certain types of food, such as meat, for the sake of the spiritual life. Some abstain from meat, some from wine or from strong seasonings or foods procured by undesirable means. For some, coffee, tea, or seasonal fruits and vegetables may fall into this category.

"Extremes meet" (*Conf.* 2.16.1) is a guiding principle. It is as harmful to eat too much as it is to eat too little. When we eat too much, we are sluggish and can fall into torpor. When we eat too little, we can also be sluggish and fall into torpor, but from a lack of nourishment rather than from digestive burdens on our system. The same thing can be said for the quality of food or drink: they can be too rich or too poor in nutrients. Both make us ill and reduce our energy for work. Most of the time people think of fasting as not eating, or eating very little with long intervals in between. We do need to refrain from eating too often, but we should not make the opposite mistake of not eating enough. Fasting is a middle way.

There are two other kinds of fasting that are rarely recommended: one is water purification fast. This fast is done by taking only water and no food for one to three days. This kind of fasting can be addictive because a "high" kicks in and our hunger subsides. Protestors often do this for one cause or another. The other kind of fast is to go on a prescribed fast, eating only what is directed by a meditation teacher. These two kinds of fasting, water purification fast and a prescribed fast, are not recommended unless you have great confidence in your director. Willfulness can trick us into using fasting as a means to pride. Even when we fast for a good cause, we should carefully examine our motives because tricks of the ego can easily get mixed in with the austerities. The means rub out merit or the desired end.

It is enough to do a consistent daily fast of the middle way except when it is time to feast or to offer hospitality. When food, for whatever reason, takes center stage it often sets the seeker inward toward self rather than further along on the spiritual journey. We may find an enormous temptation to become "food conscious" rather than to surrender to the more desirable Christ consciousness.

If fasting became a tool for our lifetime, our bodies would be tuned up for further work of the mind.

The practice of fasting:

1. Eat enough at each meal: not too much and not too little.
2. Eat the level of nutrition that gives the energy necessary for your work.
3. Eat at specified times. Refrain from eating between meals.

Exceptions to the practice:

1. Hospitality: the guest is God so provide food for them and accompany them in a shared meal.
2. Feasting: on days of celebration in the larger community eat and drink more. Richer food should be served and enjoyed. An extra time is often inserted for appetizers, a snack, high tea, or a dessert of rich quality. All this plenty marks the day with abundance and grace.

DREAMS

Even if we don't remember our dreams, we all dream. These dreams evaporate upon waking and we seem to have two levels of existence. One kind of dreams occurs during the daytime and the other during the nighttime. Just as we are not our thoughts we are also not our dreams. Even if we can't remember them, dreams are instructive for our spiritual life.

Evagrius noted that his own conversion occurred when he took an oath while he was dreaming.[5] He vowed to leave his worldly life in Constantinople and become a monk in Jerusalem. He took dreams seriously in his teachings, too. If a monk has the affliction of sex, he advises him to attend to his dreams and to see whose face emerges and if he has been using his waking time to fantasize and has therefore created an object of lust which occurs in his sleep. He says that dreams that are peaceful or only have signs of the normal needs of nature are indicators that thoughts during our waking hours are in order. But if dreams are exotic then most likely some action needs attention during our everyday consciousness.[6]

Three dream indicators signal danger: overly symbolic and chaotic sequences speak of disintegration; repetitive themes and fixations are petitions to our consciousness for attention; dark forces and directives caution us to return to prayer, since Christ has already overcome dark forces.

Welcome signs in dreams are scenes of harmony and humor: the presence of loved ones, scenes of the community of saints, and memories with little distortion. Dreams can confirm a question held with open hands before the Holy Spirit's guidance. As dreams come and go, they do hidden work in our psyche.[7]

Interpreting dreams may be dangerous because, while dreams are universal, our interpretation of them is distinctively personal. Since they do not show up in our ordinary consciousness, we should be cautious about quickly assigning a meaning to them; yet not too cautious because often, when we are ready, they reveal an important message to us.

Cassian says that a monk who is afflicted with lusty dreams should be asked what she looks like. If she's the woman in town that he's brought to the desert in his imagination, then she's no longer dwelling in town but in this very monastery. He needs to take severe measures to cut off this cycle of thoughts through the practices of guard of the heart or watchfulness of thoughts, or physical exercise or staying at the common table with the brothers.

The dream in this case acts as an indicator to the monk to not think so highly of his spiritual training and discipline that he can go to town and not suffer consequences to his inner life.

Dreams sometimes come from memories or anticipation of events yet to come. They not only mediate data and historical evidence, but they convey feelings and point to very deep levels of encounter. Daydreams, though on a lesser scale, can do the same. Everything that rises in the mind isn't core to our being, but if we are not mindful these thoughts create forces that sooner or later we have to face. Another way of saying this is that our memory, imagination, and thoughts all converge in our dreams through symbols. It's an amazing language that does two things simultaneously: puts order and restores balance in our subconscious and gives direction and focus to our conscious awareness.

Dreams are tools.[8] We can use them to view our own souls and therefore to discern how much our conscious choices are affecting our deeper unconscious ways of being true. It is a mystery that at some very deep level we are all united in a single "way of being in the world." Dreams train our un-thinking skills because all is symbol and layers and layers of mystery.

REPENTANCE

There's probably nothing more negative than to think of our past sins and regret them. But this teaching from the desert tradition has a surprising twist. The very condition that causes us to ask for help, to desire to be better, to move toward God is a gift. God loves us unconditionally. God forgives us and continues to forgive us. We need only to ask. When we do that, we stay open for the grace of forgiveness and for our faith to be restored to its original strength. We can't forgive ourselves, that's part of the problem of the human condition. We feel bad, especially we feel bad about ourselves. Guilt (even neurotic guilt, which is displaced guilt that feels as if it is one's own) should be confessed. Let God deal with it. Hand your thoughts, feelings, and passions over to our Creator to restore the right order that is imprinted on your body, mind, and soul. If we have a story to tell about the "mess" we find ourselves in, lift that up to God also. The cross is a drama. We feel divided in our hearts. We desire to do God's will but we do things we want to do. We want to love others but we love ourselves first. We hold back our real love for God and rush toward actions that satisfy us only briefly. The list is endless. Is there any way out?

Repentance is the tool. Catholics have the practice of the sacrament of reconciliation, but any Christian can take some or all of these steps. Baptism in the Catholic Church is not a prerequisite for going to confession. A heart-filled elder can do these steps, except for absolution. Absolution requires the authority of lineage. But all the other nine actions of repentance will refresh and renew us:

1. Confession: When we feel regret and wish that what we did had not happened, or wish we could redo that moment in time, we must attend to the matter. There are three conditions for sin: doing something that is wrong, knowing it is wrong, and freely consenting to do it. We've all been there. We have a story to tell and we are not proud of it. So, we need to unburden ourselves to someone. Because we are embodied we need that someone to have a face like ours and to receive this "matter." This is why our inner heart can't reconcile itself: we are "social," a "we." To root out regret another must receive our sorrow, just as to feel loved someone must love us.

One major problem with sin is denial. It takes a good deal of grace to acknowledge those three qualities of sin: matter, knowledge, and consent.

Usually we say it didn't happen, or if it did, it wasn't my fault, or if it was my fault, it wasn't so bad, or if it was bad, then I really didn't do it, it was my family of origin that made me do it—and so the cycle of victim-thinking continues. The biggest problem with that cycle is that there is no way out.

Confession is an admission that what I did (or did not do) was wrong, but I did it anyway. With this admission there is a major release of repressed energy that is worth the experience!

2. Contrition: This follows from confession, since usually we have a feeling of regret and sorrow and an accompanying feeling of being contrite. We are sad with good reason. This is a healthy sadness. Our hearts join our heads and unity is restored. If we are not sad, then we have no inclination toward good. Remorse has some "stuff" and courage is its companion. Without remorse there's no regret, no sorrow, no guilt, and most of all no responsibility.

3. Being heard: My confession needs to be heard by a caring competent human being who is ordained to give me absolution, God's forgiveness. The benefit of confession as a sacrament is similar to the manifestation of thoughts to a wise elder. Since we cannot forgive ourselves, we practice our faith by confessing to another.⁹

4. Penance: The priest asks us if we are sorry. We say yes and add that we are willing to show our true sorrow and our resolve not to repeat our sinful ways. We are then given a way to move back into our path to God. Usually we are asked to say a prayer or do a good action or speak to some person to help us take the next step toward reconciliation.

5. Absolution: We've confessed, we've been heard, and we have received a penance, now we receive absolution, the transmission of forgiveness. Absolution confirms the fact that "it" (no matter what the sin may be called: abortion, murder, rape, or fraud) is totally forgiven.

6. Making amends: As a forgiven person we must do our part to restore what we have broken. Sometimes what we did has many consequences

and we will not be able to make full restoration at one time—or perhaps ever. However, since our action to make amends shows that we wish to go in the right direction, it makes the whole of our repentance authentic.

7. Prayer: This dialogue of repentance is about our relationship with God. God saves, God forgives, God restores, God makes all things new, and God is at one with us. Therefore, conversation is appropriate between God and the soul.

8. Compunction: We have been forgiven very specific moments of sin and we know it. We are absolved and we know it. We are turned in the right direction and we know it. Nonetheless, we have sweet sorrow, mindful of the truth about us and yet grateful for God's mercy. Compunction yanks the self out of sorrow. Our spiritual senses open and begin an inner dialogue. Our inner eye of vigilance is trained on the eight thoughts. Compunction is more than ordinary repentance. Compunction is the full burden of realizing that I have done wrong and that I am experiencing God's mercy. It means to be pierced to the core of my heart. Sometimes this amazing grace of compunction is accompanied with tears that soften the heart and leave in their wake true sorrow. To receive the mystical gift of tears is rare, but those who've tasted them know they are from God and continue to cleanse, purify, and celebrate their restored relationship with God. Compunction is the most effective deterrent to pride and any form of self-love since, in compunction, there is such a radical surrender. Compunction takes us one more step toward *penthos.*

9. *Penthos:*[10] This word isn't a common one; it means having an abiding disposition of well-being, of being a restored creature. Our sadness is turned into a joy that has no comparison with any other. *Penthos* sits in the heart between the breasts. If we have this feeling, if we have experienced *penthos*—which can only be felt through our "spiritual senses"—we can no longer participate in the wrongdoings that once allured us. The disposition of *penthos* replaces the afflictions (food, sex, things, anger, dejection, acedia, vainglory, and pride). So where we had the full-blown experience of one or the other afflictive emotion, now we have the sweet sorrow of

compunction, longing for God (desire), and awareness of our being God's creature (mercy). This right relationship of truth is humility.

10. Ceaseless repentance:[11] This is the practice we must bring to our next moment of choice, when we are faced with temptation. We know what we are thinking of doing is wrong, we know we can do otherwise, but . . . and we return to our thought of ceaseless repentance. This thought usually takes the form of a prayer, "Jesus, mercy," or the whole Jesus Prayer: "Lord, Jesus Christ, have mercy on me a sinner." A daily slow, attentive recitation of the Our Father will also work toward ceaseless repentance.

Repentance makes the individual do all the work, not allowing us to wait until someone comes with an apology or till parents are gone or marriages are dissolved. If, for some reason, the external forum isn't ready for harmony—or maybe we're not ready to repent—that doesn't matter. Start now looking to God and "in faith" do all the above. This is a way to face ourselves with confidence—God's mercy will do the rest.

4

POSITIVE TOOLS

In this chapter we look at positive ways of thinking. We insert a "preferred thought" in the place of a thought we are trying to "root out." This practice has many forms. We know that the mind continuously attracts thoughts that come and go. There's no stopping them. We can learn not to notice them and do un-thinking, as we saw in the previous chapter, or we can notice the thought and substitute another thought in place of the "next" thought.

This positive practice has many tools, and we will look at five of them: ceaseless prayer, the practice of a cell, keeping vigils, manual labor, and the manifestation of thoughts. These are tools we can use while we are living alone or in a community. These are positive tools, requiring us to take action to cancel out afflicted thoughts. When we do this, we can take an action that liberates us. No one needs to use all these tools. The purpose of spiritual direction is to sort out which practices are most helpful for the individual. A monastery is simply a place where there is a tradition handing on these tools as a subculture.

CEASELESS PRAYER

In all major traditions ceaseless prayer is required of the contemplative seeker. In the Christian tradition this practice goes back to apostolic times.

The Bible commands us to "pray always" or without ceasing (1 Thess. 5:17; Eph. 6:18; and the parable of the widow in Luke 18:1–8) and makes a case that to pray intensely and with perseverance is not an attitude but a practice.

There are a variety of teachings from the monastic tradition about ceaseless prayer. They include teaching us to remember God continually through memorized texts and in-depth *lectio divina*, especially the movement of *meditatio,* or using monologistic prayer, a one-formula prayer like the Jesus Prayer, prayed over and over again. There's some debate whether the Jesus Prayer is a mantra as East Asian religions use that term. I believe it is a mantra since it is a vibratory experience that moves into deeper and deeper levels of consciousness and creates energies that effect what the words signify. The waters of baptism are actual mediums of transmission in the Eastern sense. The Jesus Prayer mantra sustains the vibrations initiated at the baptismal rite. The name of Jesus has the power to transform and sanctify.[1]

Also, we are taught to use monologistic prayers as intense prayers used in time of trial, such as, "O God, incline unto to my aid; O Lord, make haste to help me"[2] (*Conf.* 10.10.2). These short arrow-like prayers ask the heavens to reverse the patterns in our mind. Cassian devotes much of *Conference* 10 to showing explicitly how to do this, how to turn aside temptations of every kind, before sleeping, eating, going out, coming in, etc.

Later spiritual writers teach other practices to arrive at ceaseless prayer: colloquy, the Little Way, emptiness (based on *The Cloud of Unknowing* and using the little word "love" or even "sin"), practice of the presence, abandonment, or recollection. Using any of these methods causes ceaseless prayer to bear fruit: prayer happens and an abiding Presence remains.

Ceaseless prayer, which seems to reverse our mechanism of thinking and allow us to sink into deep levels of contemplation, is therefore a tool that might lead to contemplation. With experience we find that, while ceaseless prayer is continual at one level of our consciousness, nonetheless contemplation slides in, too.

The teaching about the Jesus Prayer provides the most detailed explanation of what could happen in ceaseless prayer. There seem to be three phases. In the first, or habitual phase, ceaseless prayer is practiced for short intentional periods, then increased to longer and longer periods. It stays with the same formula (we can't mix and match formulae in the initial training phase). This first phase requires strenuous effort. We know that of ourselves we can't make prayer happen, but the body and the mind need training to move into habits that are beneficial.

The second phase begins when I can notice anytime that ceaseless prayer is ongoing. This is a virtual phase where it seems "as if" the prayer is actually ceaseless. During this phase prayer has a fervor, which works on my behalf. My afflicted thoughts have a tougher time getting through. When, for example, anger, does get through, I see immediately that it is "anger" and, instead of repeating all the thoughts accompanying the passion of anger, I intentionally bring to my mind the ceaseless prayer. This virtual phase diminishes over time so imperceptibly that it's not even missed, or perhaps it stops suddenly when we are ill or undergoing some major stress. When ceaseless prayer stops, it really wasn't ceaseless, but virtual.

When that happens we start again—and again and again—making the prayer as steady as our breath. Eventually, with God's grace it becomes actual. It becomes part of our system and we do it with or without our consciousness.

Last year Sister Mary Sylvester, age 88, wanted to talk about her meditation. She had been blind for about a year and, being unsighted, took her centering prayer periods seriously. She said, "I just can't get my Jesus prayer to stop. It's going and going and keeps coming back and back." I smiled an unseen smile and took her hand and said, "Congratulations!"

Ceaseless prayer seems to me to be one among many prayer forms, but the living in the presence of God is not optional for a Christian. There are many forms of practice, but we need to respond in faith to God's presence. Ceaseless prayer is a practice that has the most weight in the Christian tradition with a literature, monastic teachings, and a full theology stored in the Christian East. A teacher is helpful, but like Sister Mary Sylvester, one can catch this prayer and have it become as natural as your own heart beat!

Manual Labor

To have a pure heart is to have a single desire (no mixture) in our heart, with no defilement or contaminants. Purity of heart is about a quality of clear light and translucent effulgence. Our heart is chaste. But it also means to be one, single, not divided or double in our intentions as in duplicity. The practice of doing one thing at a time is a first step. It is not easy to be mindful of what you are doing when you do it. To have a single intention while doing something is a practice toward single-mindedness. So, the first step is to do one thing, the second step is to be mindful of the doing of it, and the third step is to shift your intention to do it for/with/in Christ Jesus. Manual labor becomes an outward sign of inner spiritual work.

The desert tradition recommends doing ceaseless prayer as we work so that when we work this very work becomes our prayer and our prayer becomes our work. This is a reversal of the movement of thoughts that cycle and recycle back upon us over and over again so that work becomes really about "self."

When we want our work to be our prayer, doing repetitive work is easier because disciplining our mind is very difficult. When we don't have to think about how we are doing our work, we can be stable and centered.

Once we bring our mind to our work and to the doing of one thing at a time, the next step is to attend to our intentions. This is a natural flow. Since we have offered to do all for the glory and honor of God, our motivation and reason for work is all God. The guest is God, the food is Eucharist, the broom is sacred, and the computer is gift. The radical tool here, though, is not just to have "an attitude" of praising God, but an actual thought about God just as we have a thought about our work. I've had some argue that to think about God again is another thought and usually ego and not God. That's a different path, bringing God to the work. The practice of manual labor is when each touch of the hand to the device of labor is single-minded and God springs up and there's Presence. Then all is God. There is no mental overlay. Holiness emerges from underneath and we see it as it is. God is in us.[3]

This is why we need the practice of ceaseless prayer in order to do manual labor well because, when thoughts arise and take us away from doing one thing at a time and from our attention to our work, we can return to ceaseless prayer or redirect our thoughts to the mindfulness of the work at hand.

A major thief of this attentive manual work is anxiety. When we fear the future or dread consequences or regret the past, we are not attentive to the present moment. When we are anxious we need to remember God's mercy and how privileged we are to have a role in serving God. A thief similar to anxiety is an expectation of a short-term outcome. If our goal is to serve selflessly, to follow Christ even to the cross, any desirable outcome for us would be long term—a deepening love for God—not a short-term gratification of our own desires.

Silence plays a large supporting role in manual labor. If we refrain from needless chatter, silence will teach us many matters of the soul. Many times, however, our inner chatter resists silence, especially if we are undergoing the affliction of acedia (we are soul-sick and feel like spiritual work isn't worth it). However, the ancient teaching about acedia is that we should increase our time and diligence in working with our hands and body.

Eventually manual labor becomes prayer, closer to ritual than to toil. We feel the dance and begin to use the tools of our manual labor as vessels on the altar.[4] Our kitchen tools, our office set-up, and even our car become the means for attention and intention. All becomes prayer.

All of us do some manual labor but often miss its power to transform. I hear from women who do meal preparation for their family that making soup from scratch seems to be a centering prayer experience: gathering the ingredients, chopping, heating, stirring, tasting, seasoning, cooking, smelling, and keeping warm till the "act" of serving. Each moment of the event is whole in itself and requires attention, mindfulness, and calm abiding. The serving of the soup completes the ritual action with delight regardless of the response of the folks at the table.

We know we are getting the message stored in the teaching on manual labor when we expect to be asked to do the lowest task and we take it up with preference, for the sake of the spiritual life. Prestige and special attention distract us. Manual labor lends itself to the practice of humility. A sign that humility is "in process" is that we live moderately. We refrain from overworking, since truth is best served by doing just enough. Too much or too little sends us back up the chain of pride.

Since we are embodied spirits and not spirits trapped in a body, the practice of manual labor teaches us to embody our prayer. Even when we are in explicit personal prayer, it's recommended in the monastic tradition (based on biblical times) to use our bodies in prayer. We attend to our posture, as the body is the form of prayer before God. We pray with arms outstretched while the Psalms remind us to lift up our hands in prayer. The last recorded act of Christ was to lift up his hands to bless the disciples (Luke 24:50).

A mother teaching her child to pray first teaches her to join her hands and to make the sign of the Cross, as a manifestation of faith. On the High Cross in Ireland Christ's hands are nearly always emphasized and he is often shown as an *orans*. "Both your hands, O Christ, embracing me," as the Irish poet says. At Lourdes, Our Lady showed St. Bernadette how to make a proper sign of the Cross and fingered her rosary while Bernadette said the prayers.

Bows and even prostrations are prescribed in all monastic usages as well as keeping one's hands in one's sleeves or "in ceremony," while the twelfth degree of humility is mostly concerned about the body.[5]

THE CELL

The word "cell" is a monastic term. Thomas Merton influenced my understanding of this practice. The cell is a designated "personal place" for seeking God. It is a place to memorize psalms, study Scripture, a place where we can refrain from working and do our meditation. Our cell is also our bedroom, so it is designed to be a place of rest. Overwork is the biggest obstacle to seekers moving toward the kind of prayer that is absorption into God beyond images. We need an environment that will image back to us all that is or is not of God. This is why a cell is a sacred place that is kept deliberately simple.

It is a place to heal, to be comforted, and to come to wholeness. It is a place for training myself to listen; therefore, it cannot have noise that fills the silence. It must be a place where I can slow down my thoughts, where I can have a one-at-a-time experience. It is a place where "I am not my thoughts" comes home to me clearly because I see how my thoughts roam, how my moods swing, and how my feelings poke around in my imagination without consulting me. I need this personal sanctuary, a safe refuge that will help me keep my commitments, where I return to my practice of the Jesus Prayer or the colloquy or Brother Lawrence's practice of the presence. This is my bedroom, an essential place of practice where I sleep, I surrender, and I suffer the night.

I know that I'm going to die, perhaps in this very cell, so there's no running, either from this cell or from death. In the meantime the cell reminds me that I am not yet a nun/monk/spiritual person.

Can a married person have a cell especially if there is not a shared practice of prayer? I've seen some creative solutions to this dilemma. Ideally it's nice to have your partner on the same journey, but even so, there are some things one must do alone. Some have a "favorite chair" someplace else in the house that is their space, place, and solitude workbench. One sister who had to share a room with another sister simply turned her chair to the window when she wanted to "be alone." A married man told me that he put on headphones and at first listened to music, then just put them on "as if" listening and was really in silence. The cell is really the secret closet that Matthew talks about where we talk to our Father in secret (Matt 6:6). It's not really a place or a time after awhile, but an act of descending the mind into the heart and dwelling there. All of us need an external mechanism to protect our internal world.

Here's a meditation on my cell which I have based on Thomas Merton's *Contemplation in a World of Action.*[6]

"Sit in your cell and it will teach you all things." There are many variants of that teaching. I, in fact, crave a mild loneliness, an emptiness, and an exile from the world of other people. I feel a longing to go ahead and try direct confrontation with the baffling mystery we call "God."

If I'm serious about searching for God, I must undress before myself, knowing that really I'm not a nun, yet. I'm just pretending until the nun-form takes shape. I know deep down that all images of myself must be smashed and destroyed. I dread the process of unmasking my hollowness and all my illusions. They protect me from myself. But now thoughts that protect my illusions have to go.

I want to replace that deceit with the concrete reality of my vocation lived in the mysterious plan of God. I've left my cell from time to time and found nothing out there. So the place is here and the time is now.

At age fifty-seven I know that my place, the place to which I'm supposed to be tethered, is this cell. This is where I can set things in order. This is where I do my daily practice, to have no name on the door and strive to become nothing. Can I patiently put up with the incomprehensible lack of fulfillment in the lonely, confined, silent, obscure life of my cell, and gradually find my place here, the spot where I belong: in the solitude of my cell? Twenty years ago I made a retreat and truly entered into the monastic rhythm, the genius of this system. I had a mysterious awakening to the fact that where I actually am is where I belong, namely in solitude, in my cell. Suddenly I saw that "this is it."

I experienced boredom so I had to attend to my thoughts and overcome them. Some years later, in a battle with acedia, I put my eye on the real "point," the moment of truth, the aim . . . and I got my eye off achievement. I overcame my ignorance, at least for a time.

This cell is the furnace of martyrdom, just as it was for the three young children (Dan. 3).

This cell is the cloud in which God spoke to Moses (Ex. 20:21).

This cell is a fiery kiln in which precious vessels for the King are made, earth is traded for heaven (Mal. 3:2–3). My room is the workshop in which the lost likeness of the Creator is re-formed in my soul (Eph. 2:10). It is my altar where I place my gifts of fasting and contemplation (Ps. 43:3–4). "Lord grant that I may see You with a pure heart, whereas before, wrapped in my own darkness, I did not even know you." My cell is the place where I can come to know myself, but first that I can know You, my Lord. My cell (room #377) is the sole witness of the divine love flaming in the heart where I see God. And if all goes well, my cell will be like the Holy Sepulcher that alone witnessed the resurrection of the Savior on Easter morning. My cell is the place of my resurrection to divine life and light, for which I was created. According to the Irish hermit tradition, my cell will be the place of my resurrection on the last day. "Whosoever perseveres in his love of thee (O solitary cell) dwells indeed in thee, but God dwells in him."

I want now to do a further meditation based on Thomas Merton's essay on the cell that links it with the tradition of the Jesus prayer:

I sit in my cell reciting ceaselessly the Name of God. To remain in solitude with the intention of pleasing God is my delight. The Name of God is the *oratio* of solitude, allowing me to come face to face with God himself. In faith I know that the Presence of God is the Name of God. The Name of God is the Presence of God (Ex. 3:14).

This Name of God continuously prayed in my cell is God present to me. This is the whole meaning and goal of my vocation.

The Name of my God is present in the solitude of this cell as the "Son of God" was present with the children in the fiery furnace, and as the pillar of cloud (Ex. 13: 21–22) was present to Moses. This Name of God is present in my cell as in the burning bush (Ex. 3:4–6), in which YHWH revealed Himself as He Who Is . . . in faith and in this very cell is He Who Is. I invoke your Name and induce you, My Lord God, to come down to my cell in answer to my prayer.

Over time (and each year is different) my realization becomes deeper that your Name, O God, is in fact the heart of my cell, the soul of my solitary life. I am not called to meditate on your Name, but to meet Your Name. Your Name becomes, as it were, a cell within my cell, an inner spiritual cell.

When I am in my cell I recognize that I am where the Name (which has taken deep root in my heart), the Name of God Himself/Herself, is. You, Lord, cannot come to be in my cell except by my willing and loving. The Name that overshadows me in the cloud of solitude is the creative and redemptive will of your Father (Luke 1:35), and Your Name impregnates everything with a redemptive and loving significance, with promises of love and salvation, with invitations to compassion and with intercessions for everyone I know and don't know yet.

Through Your Name, O Lord God, I come to knowledge of You who make Yourself present in my solitude. You reveal your Name as that of Jesus Savior (Acts 4:10), in whom and with whom I am one with all peoples. My place as intercessor and sister is my solitude and my cell where I find and love all people in the warm and human love of the presence of Christ, for it is the Word Incarnate who alone can give me full comfort in trials that are essentially human and bound up with my physical being.

There is no peace and no reality in abstract, disincarnate, gnostic solitude. We are all hidden in Jesus Christ and therefore most intimately present to all the rest of the church (Col. 3:3). Solitude unites us all more closely in love with all the rest of humanity in the world.

In some places the Blessed Sacrament is reserved in the cell, in this very point of unity. The cell within the cell of Christ is in all of us. The secret of the cell is a paradise in which we who are called meet, in silence, the consoling and healing presence of that wisdom whose beauty is "a reflection of the eternal light and a spotless mirror of the doings of God, the image of God's excellence" (Wis. 7:26).

Vigils

To keep vigil is the state of sobriety, the opposite of being in a drunken stupor.

When we are awake, when we keep vigil, we accompany others. We join with the Holy Ones to sing the psalms before dawn and to listen to inspired Scriptures. The practice of keeping vigil is done in every Trappist Monastery. According to Charles Cummings, in *Monastic Practices:* ". . . the intention of each should be to watch for the coming of the Lord so that the hour of the master's coming will not catch us off guard like a thief."[7] He characterizes the practice of vigils as a combat or struggle—an active struggle against the powers of darkness. But the practice is also passive, an alert waiting for the dawn, a longing for the rising of the Daystar from on high. This attentive wakefulness is interior, a particular expression of the practice of guard of the heart.

Night is our common experience and like the day it, too, is sanctified by prayer, as we learn from Scripture: "That was for the Lord a night of vigil, to bring them out of the land of Egypt. That same night is a vigil to be kept for the Lord by all the Israelites throughout their generations" (Ex. 12:42).

The word translated *vigil* is the noun derived from the verb "to watch" (in Hebrew *shamor*): both in the sense of "observe" and "guard." This word is used to describe the work of shepherds. The Lord is acting as the shepherd of his people.[8]

Israel is to keep watch as it remembers God's watch during the Passover in Egypt (Ex. 12:42b). This remembrance is not merely repetition or re-enactment; it has a more active meaning of bringing something that happened in the past into the present. As the New Israel, Christians fulfill this Scripture when they keep vigil. On the other hand, it may be said that keeping vigil really means watching God watching over us.

With such strong Passover/Easter connections, ideally the regular practice of vigils should have the tone of the Easter Vigil. Keeping vigil means entering more deeply into the mystery of our redemption in Christ.

From Scripture we can see that when we keep vigil, we participate in "watching" with God to protect our turbulent world from the forces of evil that are at work.

Vigils are important in Benedict's Rule where there are no less than three chapters (out of 72) dedicated to the Night Office (Vigils).[9] The monks are to rise about two hours before sunrise. Their prayer consists of six psalms, three readings from Scripture and the Commentaries, and another six psalms. In summer when daylight is earlier, it is shorter, but no fewer than twelve psalms are sung with an alleluia refrain. On Sunday the monks rise earlier and participate in four readings, three sung canticles, and special hymns of praise. The Gospel is read, followed by the second hour of Office, Lauds. While this seems like a long vigil for Sunday, in fact Benedict modified the custom of monks staying awake all night on Saturday.

When I visit Trappist monasteries, most of the time there is one reader and the other monks are "in the dark" listening and responding to the psalms by heart. They stand only for the Glory Be to keep alert and awake, and they meditate in common. The energy in the space is palpable.

We have a natural inclination to keep vigil. Some Benedictines and Oblates do this prayer-form individually if a group isn't available. Many do the practice occasionally. There are some significant times that keeping Vigil is simply the right thing for us to do.

If I were to keep a vigil what would I do? This format is for those who have what is sometimes called a rule of life and make vigils part of their everyday life. They wake at dawn with prayer, so they must rise before the sun and be present to the dawn. Since the purpose of this prayer is to ask for blessings for the day and to ward off evil spirits of the night, most practitioners take the hour before dawn in stillness. Some do centering prayer for thirty minutes, then do a *lectio* on a current book or experience. Somehow, it seems that our natural inclination is to do intercessory prayer as the sun rises.

Another practice is to keep a vigil occasionally. Keeping a vigil is most helpful when one is in difficult times, struggling with an affliction. Some persons take an hour of vigil before sleep or when they awaken in the middle of the night. If sleeplessness happens to you occasionally, make it a vigil rather than a night of restless sleep: keep awake, use your prayer practice with total concentration, sit in silence until you feel calm and peaceful. Sometimes you may be awake the whole night. (It seems like Jesus did this from time to time also.) When we turn our insomnia into prayer, I call it staring down the night. Honest facing of our inner darkness often reverses the causes of insomnia. This occasional vigil prayer serves the same purpose as manifestation of thoughts to an elder. In this case the elder is replaced by the vigil prayer itself and we keep awake using prayers instead of manifesting the thoughts that are looping around in our mind. The psalms are a natural text for these vigils.

Another type of vigil is during an occasion of concern for another. From time to time we are called to pray intensely on behalf of another. This is the original meaning of a "wake." We stay awake and pray for another who may be dying or who is already dead. We can do this beside the bed, or the body. We can either dedicate an hour before we sleep or an hour in the middle of the night, or an hour before dawn: the method is to sit and center before an icon. Light a candle and lift up names in prayer as the Holy Spirit inspires you.

Sometimes a vigil does not emerge as a prayer form. It is simply an experience of depression. In that case, we enter into sleeplessness rather than fight it, we keep awake, we watch our thoughts come and go. It is helpful in this kind of vigil to use a prayer practice such as the Jesus Prayer. Offer the comfort of sleep and the deprivation of fatigue to those who are most in need of God's mercy. Keeping vigil is simply the response of a Christian in the cycle of darkness, whether it be night, depression, or winter. We wait, watch, and expect the light of day both physically and metaphysically. When our faith is strong the night is as the day. Dazzling darkness reveals mystery with sweet softness. No wonder lovers prefer the night.

Keeping vigil has a quality all its own. A subtle energy is stored in the wee hours of morning where stillness dances and the emerging light lifts up our spirit as dawn appears gifting us with a felt experience of joy.

Eleanor Campion answers the question "Why do you get up so early? Why do you pray at night?" She challenges her brothers and sisters who are Trappists in Ireland:

> to be ready for the Lord's return: alert, joyful, longing; to enter into the paschal movement from darkness to light; to unite in prayer with Jesus, who prayed at night; to praise God, even in darkness; to pray in darkness for and with a word in darkness; to be vigilant as an act of asceticism and penance. Perhaps someone will take this further?[10]

Manifestation of Thoughts to a Wise Elder[11]

The desert tradition includes the longstanding practice of laying out thoughts to a wise elder. This practice was the earliest form of spiritual direction. The elder would receive the manifestation of thoughts and then give the monk a word, usually from Scripture, intended to break the cycle of thoughts from going round and round in the mind. There was an admonition in the tradition "never to keep silent one's own thoughts . . . this confession is barely conceivable without tears or, if it is done with no trace of feeling, one can conclude, that it is worth very little."[12]

There is a story about Abba Zeno who was asked for his prayers. In response, he said: "Go, do not be discouraged. Say no evil of anyone and do not neglect your prayer." The other, who had asked in earnest for the prayers of the elder, told another monk: "Through the old man's prayers God has healed me." The monk replied, "As for me, it did me no good to open myself, I have not felt any effects of the cure." The one that was healed said: "And how did you beseech the old man?" He replied, "I said to him, 'Pray for me, because, I have these thoughts.'" But the first said, "While making my confession, I bathed his feet with my tears, begging him to pray for me, and through his prayers God has restored me to my health."[13]

Though this tradition of manifesting our thoughts is not often observed in our time, we can learn a great deal from it. How, for instance, do we recognize a wise elder? Would we recognize one if we saw her?

A wise elder is one who has tamed her thoughts and has compassion (meekness). This elder needs to embody the spiritual teachings in order to mediate to others the meaning of life.

If I, as a seeker, examine my conscience daily and lay my thoughts out weekly to a wise elder, which thoughts do I lay out? Most of the time I would give priority to my afflicted thoughts without analysis, then receive a short word from the elder. In response, I promise to pray for the elder and show signs of respect.

Notice the roles here, the seeker practices humility; the elder gives a discerned word. The elder gives a teaching if she intuits that the seeker is ready and willing to do the word.

If there is no wise elder available, the seeker matches inner thoughts to teachings from the tradition as they are written in a rule or in Scripture. The role of the community is to embody the teachings of the tradition so those teachings should be readily available.

A wise elder also discerns where the thoughts are coming from: self, God, or devil. She can also listen not only for the words but also for the motivations, the intentions, and the subtle thoughts that may escape the thinker. The most helpful kind of elder teaches by example as well as by words.

The seeker manifests the same thoughts over and over again as long as it takes to dismantle the affliction. The elder listens to the same material over and over again as long as it takes to reduce the afflicted thoughts, feelings, or passions.

The goal is that the seeker will notice the first inkling of a thought/emotion before it becomes a full-blown passion. To notice this moment of consent and to sharpen her will to let it go makes it easier to do the loving thing.

The elder can teach the seeker moderation. The middle way is safest. Extremes usually point to ego involvement and some pride form. Moderation is not mediocrity but surrender of the will to a higher good, God.

This relationship between the elder and the seeker is sacred. The trap of exchanging gifts should be avoided because it may lead to dependency on either side. This relationship is a spiritual gift that should have no ulterior motives.

The level of confidence in this relationship is strict and as unbreakable as the seal of confession. Like all inner-connections of the soul it should mean a relationship the seeker can count on for a lifetime.

Two questions: What happened to this practice and what would it look like today if we attempted to reclaim it?

As the eight thoughts were translated into the seven capital sins, so the practice of manifestation of thoughts became combined with confession. The logic of it goes something like this: if I'm not attentive to my thoughts, then sin gets my attention. The practice which helps me root out sin is confession or the sacrament of penance or reconciliation. If I am attentive to my thoughts, it makes sense to manifest them to someone "for help" before they coalesce into full-blown sins.

There are three major differences between manifesting thoughts, however, and confessing sins: First the nature of sin is a violation of conscience. I confess that "I did wrong." Manifesting thoughts is simply the naming of thoughts one after the other. They are rising thoughts and if identified early, often, and willingly these thoughts have very little power over my will. "I am not my thoughts."

A second difference is that, when we are manifesting thoughts, it is not recommended that we return to the past. This practice is a tool to see my thoughts "now" and to lay them out so that they have no more power over me. St. Benedict says, dash them on the rock that is Christ.[14] Confession is naming a past thought, word, or deed that was done and is now regretted.

A third difference is that confession is a sacrament that should be administered by an ordained priest. It has a history, a ritual, and a symbolic meaning that is shared by Catholic Christians.[15] The sacrament is experienced in the context of the larger ecclesial community. Manifestation of thoughts is for the on-going work of a contemplative. It's a monastic practice that is regularly done to get at the earliest level of thought and not the end-stage result of sin. The devotional confession seeks the grace of the sacrament—forgiveness of sin—manifestation of thoughts does not.

The second thing that contributed to the loss of this tradition was that the appointment of abbots and prioresses was done more and more by the reigning aristocracy and for the purpose of the administration of the monastery. The position of elder in some Eastern traditions was passed down in the non-elected role of a *staretz,* but in the West the practice of manifestation of thoughts was simply supplanted and or forgotten.[16] Can we have confidence in this old tradition from the Christian East: *exagoreusis?* St. Benedict recommended this tool.[17] It follows from the teachings on the eight thoughts that there are tools to reduce these afflictions. If there were a wise elder in our midst we would lay out our thoughts simply and humbly. We also ask her for tools that would help us.

5

SOCIAL TOOLS

The spiritual journey can be dangerous. If we become isolated, doing self-driven practices, soon the temptation is to look down on ordinary folk. Therefore, there are specialized tools we can use to keep ourselves from becoming autarchic and self-interested. These are social tools: humility, ministry, and the common table. These teachings are from the monastic tradition. I've been a nun now for forty years and find that both lay and monastic practitioners resist these social tools. I invite the reader to engage in these twelve steps of humility[1] and envision their practical implications. Ministry is the work of humble souls or it can become just another business about holy things. The common table is an actual practice where truth and love meet. These three tools, humility, ministry, and common table, become flowers in our garden if we tend to the requirements of being present in the Presence with others. We call this church.

HUMILITY

Pride is placing ourselves above others. Why is humility a social tool? Because humility is right thinking—truth—and to be truthful to ourselves and embody that truth is to be in right relationships with others. Sin is going in the opposite direction from a disciple's preferred disposition before God, humility. In that case, God takes the initiative; we receive. The Christian tradition is essentially social, not incidentally. It's faith in the "we" that mirrors the Trinity.

In chapter 7 of Benedict's Rule he pulls together from ancient sources the twelve steps of humility. You'll see that, just as these twelve steps are a recapitulation of the entire monastic rule, so the tools involved in using these twelve steps form a refrain throughout this entire book. The twelve steps are Benedict's and can be expressed in many forms, but for the sake of training in how to use the tools I've made them applicable to concrete contemporary situations.

Step One: Be aware of thoughts. We should do this with serious intentionality, because if we choose not to know our thoughts we are also saying we will not take responsibility for consenting or not consenting to our resulting emotions and passions. If these passions become sins, it is too late for prevention; at that time we need forgiveness! Thinking about being aware of our thoughts takes us back to chapters 1, 2, and 3 about becoming acquainted with afflictive thoughts. We need the tools of guard of the heart and watchfulness of thoughts to see how our thoughts come and go and how we get hooked and sometimes looped into a full-blown affliction. We need to be attentive to God's presence. This attention is more than just noticing our thoughts, feelings, and inclinations. This attention is to know that God is watching, too. There is nothing in the chamber of our inner life that is private. We are chaste only when we live in the awareness of God's presence, who is ever vigilant on our behalf.

To be attentive to God's presence is to listen, to pray, to lift up our hearts to God, and to lay aside our ever-present inner chatter. *Lectio divina* is the tool of choice to fill our hearts and mind with the Word of God rather than with our inner words and interpersonal traumas. To do this, we might memorize some of the Psalms, for instance, or know one of the Gospels in its entirety. We commit ourselves to follow the example of Christ's teaching, his healing, and his love for all. Our reference becomes Christ, the Holy Spirit instructing and filling us with an impulse to love.

Sometimes our awareness that we are in the presence of God sparks fear in us and we tremble with awed attention. The trick is to let this tremendous experience of fear be also an experience of humility. If we only back away in fear, we are refusing intimacy. We are the apple of God's eye and are held in the palm of God's hand and under his wings. Fear serves to wake us up to the awesome fact of God's love for us, which we must respond to with humility, not with denial.

We need to guard our heart and watch our thoughts. These practices are not only recommended when we are engaged in a major temptation, they are a way of living, a manner of consciousness. We have a choice to guard our hearts and watch our thoughts or not to guard our hearts and watch our thoughts. The muddy in-between states—"maybe yes," "sometimes," "I'm not sure," "it's not my practice," "I'm too busy," "some other time"—all mean that we are not guarding our heart and watching our thoughts. Just as we can't expect to pray in church if we have not prayed before we enter church, so, too, we can't expect to guard our hearts and watch our thoughts at critical times if we do not have a habit of doing that. Therefore, guard feelings, watch thoughts, be vigilant.

This awareness is a safeguard, helping us refrain from backsliding into our former way of life. We cannot be attentive to our interior life on the spiritual journey while we are living externally a life of only casual compliance with the commandments and the beatitudes. We have only one life. The inside needs to match the outside and the outside needs to match the inside. There's always tension and perhaps even combat in this dynamic, but if our outer life manifests greed, hate, and wrong relationship, then our interior life will be in service to those problems. We need to renounce our former way of life before we can start the second renunciation: that of our thoughts. When we are engaged with the forces of darkness there's no inclination to the spiritual life. And there are no short cuts: conversion comes first, sanctity second.

Step Two: Surrender our will. Conversion means turning toward God and away from self. Is it either/or? Yes, if even a part of us inclines toward evil, ignorance, and weak will, the rest of us will comply with that inclination. On the other hand, if our will is truly satisfied doing God's will, our inclination then will shift to striving toward God rather than toward evil. The Latin term *conversatio morum* (on-going conversion of my way of life) captures the in-process nature of salvation as a verb, not a once-in-a-lifetime event. This second step toward humility requires us honestly to turn from self to God, to prefer God to one's own self. This takes guts! There is enormous resistance to taking this step and it needs to be practiced over and over again because we will take our consent back, over and over again.

The tools to help us keep this resolve are ceaseless prayer, vigils, and fasting. I can tell if a person is ready for this if they understand the wisdom of renunciation as a way of life. Restraint and disciplined training have a positive energy! Using discipline and restraint is no longer an imposition from the outside, but a wonderful and liberating way to live. It's an easy way of breathing that replaces that breathless hustle of living for the self.

Step Three: Be accountable to another. Once we know our weaknesses, we need help. The nature of thoughts is that in the mind they can loop around and come up to the will as a good idea. Often only someone from the outside can inform us clearly that they are not. In secrets there are lies. Our inclination to evil will be checked early, often, and completely if we manifest our thoughts to a wise elder. Not only can we reduce, redirect and root out our afflictions, we can check and redefine our motives. Sometimes, if there is sin, we need the sacrament of penance. Other times we can strive against sin in the groups that we belong to. Ultimately we need to be accountable to someone or some group about our things, our relationships, and our manner of life. A group that embodies the teachings we are striving to live helps us keep our promises and shows us ways to live authentically in our culture, ways to imitate Christ.

In this third step we see the value of submitting to authority. This submission has specific requirements. We hand over our independence for the sake of direction. We submit. This submission is not simply an attitude. It is an admission that we are influenced not only by ourselves, but by the "other," whether in marriage or in religious community or in our life as a single person within the human community. An understanding that this is so is essential for spiritual well-being. Since God is not visible and since we fulfill God's commandments through social constructs, we must submit to someone and some pattern as if it were God herself giving the commands. It's not so important what those commands are, as it is to submit. To bind the will. To lay aside one's agenda for the sake of another. The directive is to become obedient even to death (Phil. 2:8). We accept suffering as redemptive. We empty ourselves.

In a day of widespread abuse of authority and stress on independence and self-worth, this step is particularly difficult. But we must find a way to accomplish it for the sake of training in spiritual maturity. This training shows us why the directive on anger is so clear and compelling. If we train ourselves to be angry at any contradiction of our inclinations and will, we will be hopelessly far from the strength to practice this third step of humility.

Step Four: Carry out difficult tasks without weakening or going away. We must embrace suffering. Unless we carry out difficult tasks that go against our preferences, we only shore up our ego; we return to the self by doing what we want, when we want to do it. But what if what is asked is evil, or useless, or beneath our dignity? The steps of humility get more difficult as truth filters through our nervous system. We are told to expect sacrifice and to anticipate hardships. We are to turn the other cheek, give our only cloak, and go the extra mile (Matt. 5:39–41). Is this literally true? Yes, this is the tradition of renunciation and imitation of Christ: the Christian way as outlined in the Acts of the Apostles.

Step Five: Manifest thoughts to a wise elder. This is a specific directive. I will quote it in its entirety:

> The fifth step of humility is that a monk does not conceal from his abbot any sinful thoughts entering his heart, or any wrongs committed in secret, but rather confesses them humbly. Concerning this, Scripture exhorts us: Make known your way to the Lord and hope in him (Ps. 37:5). And again, Confess to the Lord, for he is good; his mercy is forever (Ps. 106:1, Ps. 118:1). So too the Prophet: To you I have acknowledged my offenses; my faults I have not concealed. I have said: Against myself I will report my faults to the Lord, and you have forgiven the wickedness of my heart (Ps. 32:5).[2]

Given this strong directive from the *Rule of Benedict* it seems compelling that we shift our emphasis from confession of sins to manifestation of thoughts. This tool would prevent sin and keep us living in the present moment.

Step Six: Practice manual labor. There's little contemporary support for this practice, since the teaching is to prefer menial treatment, even to be ignored rather than praised. The practice of manual labor is a tool that teaches us to stay content with what is and, if there's a preference, even to take a lower level of recognition rather than a higher level. Humility is truth and usually we have a tendency to place ourselves above others and in an exalted position rather than being of service. The Christian way is to serve and to take the path for the sake of the other and the least reinforcement for the ego. Humility is truth. We don't create another commentary around what is.

Step Seven: Consider it a blessing if one has been humiliated and dismissed. This takes the sixth step even further. But if we do it, what keeps us from simply wallowing in low self-esteem? Our ego seems to have been damaged by early formation or deformation. Psychology teaches that in our formation infants first develop a sense of self and then later, as adults, a sense of self-esteem, and that they ultimately transcend that sense as they move toward others and toward God. The early desert elders taught that we first have a right relationship with God, self, and others. Then we participate in original and personal sin and lose that relationship. However, grace is offered to us and, as we respond to grace, we are able to change our ways, leave our former way of life (which is rooted in original and personal sin), and embrace the cross. The Eastern traditions have a description that involves the theory of karma and reincarnation. Each act has its consequences and we will have as many lifetimes as it takes to evolve beyond our human condition to reach nirvana or realization. Are these just different words for the same process?

It seems to me that all three theories have their problems. If we rely on the self-development theory, self becomes the goal of life. If we rely on desert spirituality, we can become discouraged and possibly depressed if we don't have a wise elder. If we rely on Eastern ways, we miss the distinctive Christian immersion in Christ and the cross.

So, it seems to me that the starting place is Christ rather than our own development. We must throw ourselves unconditionally upon our Creator and follow the impulses of grace. God made us and we will return home full of light, related to the whole cosmos and to each other. My body, my mind, and my way of living this life are sanctified through Christ Jesus.

Step Eight: Be content with what is. We are not so special that we have to "go it alone." The common life will do it for us. This doesn't mean mediocre and banal living but to have common sense while doing ordinary things. The real is holy and those who have gone before us and are travelling alongside of us are our guides. Humility receives another's truth and puts it into practice in her own hour-by-hour agenda and to-do list. This practice of humility yields peace as our desires are quieted and the moment's blessings are enough.

Step Nine: Restrain talk and remain silent. We often regret what we say but seldom offend anyone by our attentive silence. To know silence we must refrain from talk. Then, as we know silence further, we can refrain also from inner chatter!

Step Ten: Laugh only when you are in the same camp. Often laughter is at or against another. When we are loud, boisterous, joking, there is danger of placing ourselves above another person and putting him or her down. Lack of humility prompts us to target another and ridicule, scorn, disdain, or satirize them to bolster our own ego.

Step Eleven: Speak straight, "as is." Do not speak of yourself as *up*, that is vainglory, nor *down*, that is dejection. And do not make fun of another nor depreciate them in thought, word, or deed.

Step Twelve: Recapitulate the above directives. Let routine teach us patience and the rhythm of grace. Prefer silence to talking about one's self. Prefer sincerity to laughter. Make our speech direct, soft, reverent, kind, and truthful. If we do, it will show in the posture of our bodies. We will walk with poise, receptive and willing to serve. Through the practice of humility we simply come to know ourselves, and that has an immediate corollary. We have no right to judge another.

The fruit of humility is that, through self-forgetfulness, we abide in the presence of God.

MINISTRY

While along the way we may feel a surge of zeal, we cannot appoint ourselves for ministry. If we do, two problems ensue: first, we may be doing this public work out of a motivation of vainglory; second, we might harm others in the name of God.

Motivation is critical. We must refrain from public ministry for our own self-growth, or perhaps from the therapeutic end of getting over depression or adversity. Ministry cannot be one's "outlet." We need to refrain from ministry if we are afflicted with thoughts of anger (we would have no discernment or light for others), depression (we will ask those we serve to serve the wounded healer), acedia (we will take ourselves and our flock toward superficial accomplishments rather than God), or any other affliction that hinders the work of the Holy Spirit. In short, the harm done to others is that they trust us in good faith to mediate Christ and, in turn, we export our afflictions.

All of us are called to work on behalf of others, but few are called to ministry, that is, called in the name of the church, to serve others, as Christ.

We must be called to a particular place, or group, or designated institution. This call must be an authorizing one: This means that the caller has the authority to designate us, name us as minister, and send us to a particular service. If we are called, we are judged to be worthy, qualified, and competent to serve, no longer in our own name, but in the name of the church. We do not authorize ourselves. Even Christ was baptized, given a confirming sign of the Holy Spirit, and did only the work of his Father.

In the light of the desert tradition, there are twelve practices that guide us in ministry:

1. We must strive to be free from afflictions that diminish our effectiveness. Our right effort is to change ourselves. This will change others.

2. We must guard against vainglory and ascribe all good done to the glory of God and not to oneself. We must refrain from daydreaming , making ourselves the hero, the object of glory. We must speak truth without embellishment or boasting. We must check our motivations about the work and refrain from seeking self-gain, promotions, higher callings, more recognition, or inflated standing among peers or superiors.

3. We are to accept our limitations without dejection. Limits prompt us to ask for help and to try again with God's mercy. We must refrain from thoughts of "unworthiness" or *down* thoughts. They are actually a form of pride because you really think you are better than you are. Therefore, we must refrain from self-talk that puts others down or up. Humility is truth.

4. Our call requires us to submit in obedience to the authorizing officials of the church or the institution that designates where, when, and with whom we are to be of service.

5. The heart of the work is to serve selflessly, wholeheartedly, not counting the cost and without seeking results. We must replace self with faith.

6. To do this we accept the grace of the moment and facilitate the self-determination of others. We put others' good ahead of our own. We sacrifice. If there are side effects to this sacrifice we surrender the resentment that may rise when our needs are not met.

7. When it's time to move on, we do. Though usually in ministry the work is never done, often our little part of it is completed. We must remember that our ministry is an appointment. So there is a time for "dis"-appointment as well. Termination of services is to be expected when the authorizer matches the needs of the community with the gifts of the minister. We must respect the gifts of others and pray for those with whom we differ.

8. We wisely refrain from using any form of domination or oppression which distances us as minister from the needs of those being served. Regularly we must check our use of entitlements, of time, dress, gait, and patterns of communication. We strive to be attentive listeners, to be in service to the other and not to the self.

9. We accept no gifts and give no gifts in exchange for spiritual work. This sets up too many opportunities for ulterior motives. If we are a "professional," the institution must provide the exchange, not the individual "customer." Ministry is a delicate work that can ill afford to appropriate risky business practices.

10. There is, however, a return to the minister from the "flock." We participate in ministry in such a way that we ennoble others. In that way, we receive the others' gifts intended by the Holy Spirit for our salvation.

11. We accept mistakes we make as part of everyday life. We forgive, forget, and move on. We are not surprised at our weaknesses. This awareness makes us more reliant on God rather than ourselves.

12. Finally, we hold in prayer each and every one we serve. Sometimes this takes the form of praying literally in the stead of the person who cannot pray at his or her time of need.

The practice of ministry is not everyone's calling for a lifetime. Some are called for some years, or for one task, or to a special group. The benefit of being called, named, and sent by an authorizing person (bishop, priest, or abbot) provides a safe path for us.

THE COMMON TABLE

Another social tool that we take for granted in service of the spiritual life is the common table. The discipline to stay at common table outdistances even the most seasoned contemplative. The common table can be of enormous benefit for all of us. Immediately, you may say, "I live alone," or, "My schedule is different from the family," or, "My community life has shifted. Now each person must go to the cafeteria on her own schedule." I invite the reader to envision how this teaching would be helpful for your spiritual life.

No matter what the circumstances, eating is a social moment. We communicate with our food, plant life or animal life. We pause, give thanks, and attend to this food that brings nourishment and well-being. More than that, all of us eat at the common table of planet earth. There is a case to be made for literally and specifically eating "in common" at the common table. We keep our feet on the ground and we sit upright, face to face with another or others. This opportunity to share food from common bowls and platters is an excellent image that we are not alone. We need others and others need us.

The spiritual life can spin into unreality if we eat mindlessly, work incessantly, sleep fitfully, and talk at each other. To reverse this kind of living, we should use the tool of the common table: eat mindfully, slowly, with poise and manners. We wait for food to be served, take what is given, and are grateful. Eating at a designated time is part of our tool of fasting. We stop our work to eat, so food and others have our full and undivided attention. We eat much like we prefer to sleep, that is, to take whatever time it requires to be rested and balanced. The most challenging aspect in the practice of the common table is facing another. When we face one another, others reflect to us what they need and how we can be helpful. They want to be heard and welcomed at table. They want to know that part of your day will always be shared with them and they can count on your presence.

Common table is a smaller replica of the Eucharistic table. We continue the celebration of the Mass in our dining rooms. In 1995 when four of us, all monastics, went to India, Nepal, and Tibet, we were struck by the fact that Buddhist monks and nuns have no tradition of common table. Their goal is to study how to be enlightened, so they sometimes eat, even in the main temple, so that they do not have to interrupt their chanting. Is eating the way we eat, therefore, just a Western cultural tradition? In Christian monasticism, at least, it is an essential part of the way of life in common.

In many monasteries today silence is still observed in the refectory. One monk reads while the rest eat. This reading has a calming effect and is quite social. Talking is not the only way of sharing. We soon find that in silence levels of experience are shared that bind a group together beyond many conversations that sometimes keep us apart. When we do converse after table reading, there is a text to talk about that furthers our spiritual quest.

A common rule in every household and monastery is that if you live there you are entitled to take food at the table. Conversely there's a rule that, if you are absent, there had better be a good reason. Absence takes you away from the goal of relationship. Sometimes in monastic life a nun out of relationship with the community absents herself from the table. This always creates concern and we make a special effort to welcome and invite her back.

Common table is a social tool to keep us in the here and now—with real people, with real problems. The value of this social tool cannot be overestimated. It has a powerful ability to keep the seeker turned toward others rather than toward herself and turned, as well, toward the larger concerns of our church and world. This social tool has not been surpassed in bringing order to our day, gratitude to our hearts, and kindness to our ways. We awake with the dawn and bow to others instead of the sun.

6

PRAYER TOOLS

Negative Prayer Tools (Apophatic)

THE JESUS PRAYER (PRAYER OF THE HEART)

The Jesus Prayer is the traditional practice of ceaseless prayer in the Christian tradition. The usual form is "Jesus, Son of God, have mercy on me, a sinner." The longer form is "Jesus, Son of the Living God, have mercy on me, a sinner."

Several shorter forms are "Jesus, have mercy on me," or "Jesus, mercy" or "*Kyrie Eleison.*" The shortest form is simply "Jesus."

When this prayer is practiced over time, it drops into the heart and becomes the prayer of the heart. The teaching is rich. The invocation of the Holy Name of Jesus, which continues our baptismal immersion, brings our attention to Christ and Christ, in turn, dwells in us. The prayer warms the heart and becomes an experience of Presence. In the Christian East a *staretz* would caution the pilgrim that doing this prayer takes assiduous practice. But the Jesus Prayer can become ceaseless and self-acting with training.

The training in how to practice the Jesus Prayer has three stages:

- toward a habit by committing the prayer to memory
- toward a spontaneous mental prayer
- toward a self-acting continuous prayer

To make it a habit we must say the words slowly, mindfully, and with respect for their meaning. We do this repetition at specific times with a certain number in mind, somewhat like repeating the prayers of the rosary, fifty times in five sets. Then we rest and repeat it another fifty times in five sets. We do this morning and evening for two weeks. Then we increase it, repeating the words one hundred times in two sets, morning and night. After several months we add another set of one hundred repetitions in three sets, adding one at midday.

Notice we don't use the word "sit." The Jesus Prayer is a "working" prayer done as we do other things. It is not a meditation practice like centering prayer. The centering prayer method uses the "sacred word" only when a thought arises. The Jesus Prayer is cultivated ceaselessly; we concentrate on making it happen while we are doing our ordinary tasks of walking, driving, cleaning, cooking, managing children, or teaching a class. We keep increasing our repetitions gradually until we start to feel the prayer rising automatically in the in-between times. If for some reason we stop our practice, we start it again with three sets of fifty repetitions. After about two months (sometimes I've known people who have passed the first stage in two weeks), this ceaseless Jesus Prayer will be self-acting all the time.

The next stage is spontaneous or virtual. The prayer continues for several months, even years, though in adversity or through lack of mindfulness it may drop from consciousness. If this happens—because this habit was only virtual, not actual—we simply start again, doing the strenuous effort of making it a habit again. Usually the second or third time is easier. Often when we are in a period of affliction, when we need the prayer most, it goes away. It simply must be brought back to the afflictive thought of food, sex, anger, and so on. Therefore, in practice the Jesus Prayer goes on continually, but especially when we are challenged with a temptation or an inclination that takes us away from our resolve.

The final stage is self-acting or "actual." The Jesus Prayer actually is praying itself! I don't know of anyone fully in this stage. While we are in this life, we must always be vigilant that our prayer be constant, so we cannot count on this. We can fall away anytime. However, God's grace is stronger. If the prayer stops, we simply and gently start again and it returns to its place in our consciousness.

Eventually the words have an automatic cadence that starts to follow our breath. Sometimes the Jesus Prayer is called the "breath prayer" since it is in sync with one's breathing: we inhale saying, "Lord, Jesus Christ," then pause, saying mentally, "Son of the Living God," and then exhale saying, "have mercy on me, a sinner."

With practice the breath itself becomes the prayer—with no words. The breath carries our intention. In English the formula is long so some find it easier to shorten the formula to "Jesus, Mercy" or "*Kyrie Eleison.*" The repetition should be slow, soft, and quiet. Gentle, like a feather, since this is anointing the soul and celebrating the Presence.

The Jesus Prayer comes from the lips through the mind through the breath to the heart and becomes the prayer of the heart. This third phase is more a gift than an intentional effort. It usually happens on retreat or at times of protracted quiet. The prayer of the heart happens when we find that place in our heart where "rest" happens—that is contemplative prayer beyond thought.

Even though it's usually a by-product of the Jesus Prayer, once we've experienced the prayer of the heart we can descend to that place at will. During this traditional practice, our gaze descends to our heart while we experience in faith that God is gazing at us. Our mind's eye is in the physical/spiritual heart. We give attention to the heartbeat that carries the intent of the Jesus Prayer. In Eastern Christianity this prayer is practiced while gazing at an icon.

It is important to know that if we accompany the Jesus Prayer with a breath or a heartbeat in prolonged periods in an intensive sitting method, we need a spiritual director or an elder who is experienced in this practice. It is so powerful that our life takes on a more demanding spiritual sensitivity.

The companion practice in ordinary waking consciousness is guard of the heart. We rededicate ourselves to guard of the heart and watchfulness of thoughts while we recall the memory of him whom we are experiencing in our very being.

The teachings continue to say that the prayer of the heart is practiced ceaselessly, as was the Jesus Prayer, but instead of mentally invoking the name we practice warming the heart with love.[1]

The Jesus Prayer/Prayer of the Heart is assisted by using a rosary (or prayer-rope) so that the person can physically use the whole body, when walking, waiting, or sitting in a designated prayer period.

The Jesus Prayer is portable and is meant to be done in all your waking time. It is most helpful to do upon awakening and before sleep. Even when we are in our first training we need not "sit" and meditate on it. We can do it while driving, walking, waiting, or doing dishes. It's an active prayer. Some teach that in initial stages it is helpful to concentrate and dedicate a few minutes, perhaps ten here and there, in order to say the Jesus Prayer with full attention. But I find that, if folks wait to reorder their life to get those ten minutes of attention, they never get started. So, just start where you are with whatever you are doing. It is especially helpful to do during manual labor that is repetitive and doesn't need your whole attention.

Some worry, if they are doing the Jesus Prayer, how much of their mind will be "left-over" for attentive work, like computer tasks, teaching, or social work. When the mind needs to be attentive to other work, the Jesus Prayer will drop down in consciousness and the brain will activate a clear mental process for the business at hand.

The benefit of the Jesus Prayer is that, while we are doing manual or mental work, we are more attentive since the "mantric" prayer is at work reducing unwanted distractions and aiding our concentration. The effects of the eight thoughts are reduced. Our mind is at peace. This actually frees our conscious mind to be more receptive to whomever we are listening to.

The fruit of the Jesus Prayer is that it becomes the prayer of the heart and an abiding presence of God. This presence is usually apophatic: no image, no concept, it just is! Yet there is an experience of the presence that you feel with your "spiritual senses." The Jesus Prayer does not replace other forms of prayer such as the Divine Office or the Liturgy of the Eucharist; however, it is the unifying prayer that brings to life the other prayer forms that are part of our specific vocation.

Even in dryness, this prayer has no heaviness, no languishing, and no struggling. It has a life of its own that is an experience of emptiness. Instead of aridity, a feeling of compunction—longing for God but being separated from God—rises. The words of the Jesus Prayer and its disposition prevent dejection, vainglory, and pride. Our heart is like a boat coming into safe harbor, the harbor of humility.

Can everyone do it? While everyone can do this prayer, not everyone is called to it. We know we are called to it if these four conditions are present: (1) we feel drawn toward the invocation of the Name; (2) we see that the practice produces in us an increase of charity, purity, obedience, and peace; (3) we find the use of other prayer practices becoming somewhat difficult; and finally (4) we find that the Jesus Prayer simplifies and provides a unity to our spiritual life.

The practice of the Jesus Prayer will thrive unless one sins. If that happens, we must return immediately without hesitation. If we resume the practice it will be an aid to resist temptation in the future. The request for mercy is real. *Penthos* is an abiding state of remaining in the need of God's mercy. With spiritual practice comes a clear, focused mind. When we have a sense of being in need of God because of being a sinner, we feel a real sense of *penthos* or compunction.

A fuller explanation and teaching about this tradition of the Jesus Prayer is stored in the Christian East, especially in the writings of the *Philokalia*.[2] The Jesus prayer is rooted in Scripture and we can accompany our practice of it with *lectio* on the Scripture passages.

The dominant fruit of this practice of the Jesus Prayer that becomes prayer of the heart is the experience of a moment, a place, a space of contemplation. A profound silence brings together our fragmented mind and we become stable and attentive. After years of practice we can descend our mind into our heart "at will" and find that place of stillness (*hesychia*).

THE PRACTICE OF EMPTINESS
(THE CLOUD OF UNKNOWING)

As befits the title of his work, the author remains anonymous despite much speculation about his identity.[3] Most theories suggest that he was a Cistercian hermit or a Carthusian priest. Regardless of his status, his writing reveals a keen theological mind and he was obviously a perceptive director of souls. His teaching reflects the negative or apophatic spiritual tradition which emphasizes that God is beyond thoughts, concepts, and images. The author is believed to have lived in the East Midlands, a region of central England, during the latter half of the fourteenth century. He contributed to an exceptional wave of spiritual literature emerging from England at that time, including the works of Richard Rolle, Walter Hilton, and Julian of Norwich. In addition to his spiritual teaching, the unknown author is highly regarded for his literary gifts. His work displays remarkable strength and vigor in its original Middle English. Six other anonymous works are attributed to this author; probably the most well known of these is "A Letter of Private Direction" (often entitled The Book of Privy Counseling.) *English-speaking readers seem to have an affinity with the Middle English in which he wrote, reporting that* The Cloud *reads like an inspired book of Scripture.*

We are all called to contemplation, to rest in God. There are many paths to this end. The path specifically taught by the author of the *The Cloud of Unknowing* is for those attracted to the mystery of God but who are not inclined to go through images of Jesus or Mary or through the life of Jesus Christ as devotion. Their attraction is Christ-centered, but without images and stories. The author speaks for those of us who prefer the apophatic (imageless) path when he speaks of God as a jealous lover. We fix our love on him. Close the doors and windows on imagination because God is beyond our thoughts, concepts, and images.[4] The teaching of the method is helpful and easy to understand, but hard to do. The practice is to lift up your heart to the Lord with a gentle stirring of love, desire him for his own sake, not for his gifts. Center all your attention and desire on him. Let him be the sole concern of mind and heart. We need to forget all else. Feel nothing else but a kind of darkness about your mind. This is the Cloud of Unknowing.[5]

We can't will ourselves to feel naked before God, but we can practice a naked intent toward God. If we simply stay with the teaching, the meaning will emerge. The practice is delicate and subtle but intelligible.

The teaching goes on to say, "Though we cannot know him we can love him. By love he may be touched and embraced, never by thought. . . in the real contemplative work you must set all . . . aside and cover it over with a cloud of forgetting. Then let your loving desire, gracious and devout, step bravely and joyfully beyond it and reach out to pierce the darkness above. Yes, beat upon that thick cloud of unknowing with the dart of your loving desire and do not cease come what may."[6] Place your hope in feeling and seeing God as he is in himself. This is a negative path: we un-think what we think about God so that God emerges in our thoughts as God is and not as we wish or fabricate God to be.

When we cry out to him whom we love, we do it often and always in this cloud, this darkness. We forget all else. This isn't just a pious recommendation; this is a request literally to forget all thoughts racing in our minds. In exchange, we receive God who brings us to deeper levels than ordinary surface consciousness. We come to a deep experience of God himself.

The unknown author gives us a method that was taught one thousand years before he was writing in the fourteenth century. He tells his seekers to choose a single word, one syllable, but one that is meaningful to you. The word might be "God" or "love." Fix it in your mind so that it will remain there, come what may. He tells his seekers to use this word to "beat" upon the cloud of darkness above (the beat is more like the baton of an orchestra leader, a steady beat, soft, measured, not like a baseball bat). This is how you enter the cloud. Now all of us have thoughts rising from below. What do we do with them? He recommends that to subdue all distractions, move them, consign them, to the cloud of forgetting beneath you.

Answer with your word alone to any thought that enters your consciousness. Think not about the thought. The value lies in the simplicity (oneness) of your consciousness. Contemplation is a way of knowing where one turns to God with a burning heart, desiring only God and resting in blind awareness of one's own naked being.

From my study of the desert tradition, this is how I understand this practice:

We want to move into the third renunciation, that is, to renounce even our thought of God, because just as we are not our thoughts, neither is God our thought of him. So we take whatever level of purity of heart we have and walk between the Cloud of Unknowing (because we can't know God by thought) and the Cloud of Forgetting (because we often bring all our distractions to that little word of love that carries our intent of love). We repeat the word over and over, without thinking any particular thought.

We love God only for his own sake. We use the image of a cloud (non-thought) and, using the sacred word, enter the Cloud of Unknowing by practicing in the Cloud of Forgetting nothing else but a naked intent to love.

Like most practices, this will make more sense when it is part of your experience. Descriptions fail to capture the simplicity and profundity of this "Way of Unknowing." We also attend to Scripture. We do *lectio*, sitting easily, using the words of Scripture like a mirror. The words reflect God and draw us into mystery. On this path, we are particularly attracted to the unitive sense of Scripture in the Gospel of St. John or in John's Epistles. We pray intuitively not analytically. We let what comes arise and stand before us. This is not the study of a scholar. Let prayer rise, a short prayer that pierces the heavens.

During prayer we forget the self. By letting go (or letting be without accompanying a thought with another thought), we empty our minds and hearts of everything except God during the time of this work. We refrain from other kinds of knowledge and from processing other experience. We want no less than God, trampling everything else beneath the Cloud of Forgetting.

In this kind of prayer brute force has no place. We come like a child. Our heart waits for the gracious initiative of the Lord. And God comes, like our naked intent, quietly. We usually have no experience of consolation or desolation. We find consolation only in doing God's will. If I can name one word that describes the experience of this kind of prayer it is "subtle." There are simply hints of the sacred. We must be alert to receive them but without any expectation. We are letting God be God and letting faith be faith.

Sometimes when we talk about prayer we use words like "lift up our hearts" or "put our thoughts down in the Cloud of Forgetting" or "move into contemplation" or "out in gratefulness." All these words must be erased. They limit God. We often describe God as too small, narrow, absent or out there. We must refrain from thinking this way in the practice of the cloud. Even the cloud can't be taken as a literal image. Another way of describing this particular prayer method is the practice of emptiness. We un-think but warm our hearts and send the word as darts of love. The stress on warming our heart is a later tradition and serves as a corrective to not relating with others, since this prayer practice is so impersonal.

Formlessness, however, doesn't mean being bereft of spiritual and full-bodied warmth toward God and toward others. No words can fully describe this awesome way of prayer. All prayers, but particularly the practice of emptiness, stress desire, not results. We never get there; it is simply a way of being before God. To be there (before God) we discipline the imagination so that we are not mentally someplace else! Our ordinary senses are not up to this level of receptivity, so we must distrust our senses whenever we fix our minds on an image that represents God.

As we walk, our thoughts can safely pray this prayer: "That which I am I offer to You, O Lord, without looking to any quality of Your Being, but only to the fact that You are as You are; this, and nothing more. That which I am, I offer to You, O Lord, for You are it entirely. . . . That I am . . . that You are."[8] I know of nuns who do this emptiness practice using the mantra, "That I am, that You are."

The author of *The Cloud* says, "Go no further, but rest in this naked, stark, elemental awareness that you are as you are."[9] You must stand at the door of contemplation and practice devotion of heart. Using your word, send your naked intent to Our Lord in the Cloud of Unknowing.

We said that there are many paths and not everyone is called to walk the same path. Here are signs of this calling to contemplative prayer.

1. You will notice a growing desire for contemplation—a blind longing of the spirit—constantly intruding into your daily devotions. This longing lingers after your time of prayer, and a kind of spiritual sight awakens which both renews the desire and increases it. This desire is blind (it comes from underneath). If you are still processing your sins or working out the consequences of Our Lord's passion in your own life, you still need the ordinary way of prayer and not a more intense life of grace.

2. You manifest a certain joyful enthusiasm welling up within you whenever you hear or read about contemplation. Nothing else satisfies. Your inclination to desire a way of prayer rather than simply saying prayers persists. If your contemplative longings capture and intrude on all you do and are there when you wake up and go to sleep, then it is a call to contemplative prayer.

For those called to the practice of emptiness, the contemplative bent described above is present, but they also are detached from any prayer practice that uses images or thinking. For some, the opposite experience is to be invited to a colloquy in which there is a continual conversation with Our Lord. Emptiness practice is generally wordless. But like all contemplative practices, there may be a phase when Our Lord takes over and even words become rest!

THE LITTLE WAY OF ST. THÉRÈSE OF LISIEUX

Thérèse of the Holy Child Jesus was born Marie Françoise Thérèse Martin in 1873 in Alençon, France, into an intensely devout family who nurtured her profound spiritual awareness. Thérèse's mother died when she was four years old and for the next eight years she struggled with an overly sensitive and timid nature. On Christmas Day 1886, before her thirteenth birthday, she was released from her emotional weakness and received the gift of "love and a spirit of self-forgetfulness." Thereafter she prepared to become a Carmelite and obtained hard-won permission to enter the Lisieux Carmel at the age of fifteen. Rejecting the extreme penances common at this time, Thérèse practiced unspectacular self-denial, recognizing that everyday events have spiritual value. Her final illness and death in 1897 at the age of twenty-four was marked by physical suffering and excruciating spiritual darkness which she endured for souls without faith. She wrote fifty-four poems. Her autobiography, The Story of a Soul, *is a compilation of three manuscripts written from 1895 to 1897. In it she describes her "Little Way" of recognizing our nothingness and offering the depths of our poverty to God, expecting everything from God and trusting in his merciful love.*

The Little Way is offering our very self to merciful love. We need not be perfect. It is sufficient to present ourselves to God as we are. The depth of his mercy is attracted to the depth of our poverty. Instead of relying on our own spiritual accomplishments, we must rely only on the strength of him. Eternal life to those who believe was the promise of Jesus. Our responsibility is to believe that this is true and live our lives accordingly. The Gospel events have energy to sustain us in this pursuit of the ordinary way, the Little Way of being a saint. God rewards littleness if we bear with ourselves in spite of our imperfections. The Little Way is a short, quick, straight way, an urgent need to fulfill our desire to be one with God. "Whoever is a little one, let them come to me."[10]

The Little Way is premised on an image of a mother holding a child. The arms of Jesus lift the child up to the mother. The smaller you are the easier it is to lift you up. The gift of littleness is that we become light, not weighed down by anxiety, guilt, dread, and heaviness. Littleness cuts the bonds that drag us down. When we are little, we expect everything from God. We let go of anxiety, fear, and self-centeredness and rely only on God. We have nothing. God is all. So we own, accept, and face our nothingness. The "little" part of the Little Way is all about nothingness. The "way" part is about renouncing attachment to my emotions or feelings. Even when my desires are dried up, this ache after God is part of the littleness I experience.

In *lectio* with St. Thérèse's writings, I learned that she was like her teacher, St. John of the Cross, apophatic to the core. Yet, the nineteenth-century feminine version of this sixteenth-century master of the spiritual journey required a degree of severity in her prayer: no thought, no emotions and affect, no feelings of self-centeredness, simply ordinary life. She refrained from feeling sorry for herself; in fact, she refrained from feeling anything. She offered her emotional life to God and returned all feelings of love in "faith" toward God.

So, the "way" in the Little Way is all about renouncing emotional satisfaction and giving all love to God. A welcome feature of the Little Way is that there is no disdain of creatures. Rather, loving God enabled her to love much. Nothingness was a brilliant way to restrain herself from any illusions, any false expectations of a return on emotional investment. To get at the uniqueness of this path, we only have to think of the brilliance of St. John of the Cross renouncing all thought of God in prayer and undergoing the dark night to let God be God in his soul. In St. Thérèse we have a renunciation of affect. She would say of herself she never let herself take a vacation from giving all. To preempt the question of repressed emotions, it is clear that in her nothingness she already dealt with anger, depression, and the drag of the human condition. She understood that she was really and truly nothing. Therefore, for her to renounce emotions would simply be to embrace truth. She had no ego-consciousness to nurture. She literally preferred nothing to Christ.[11]

How did she reach such heights? For her First Communion St. Thérèse performed 1,949 sacrifices, or 28 each day. She repeated an invocation 2,773 times or 40 times a day.[12] This concentration on counting acts prepared her to move into an habitual way of living away from herself, giving herself over to the impulse of grace to give all to God. She had a way of seeing Christ's holy face and his agony on the cross "in faith," uttering those real but also symbolic words, "I thirst." She saw the practice of sacrifice uniting her to Jesus, and she participated in his act of redemption of others. She even saw the value of substituting her life for another's. This was her prayer when she prayed for Pranzini's conversion before his execution. For her, faith was seamless. Ask and it shall be given even if it be the salvation of a sinner.[13] All will be granted through God's mercy.

Suffering for her was the way to transmute desire. Her desire was one thing only, always to suffer for Jesus. It is through suffering we can save souls and these souls praise God for all eternity. So, suffering and adoration were the same act.

We know that in this Little Way Thérèse had genuine love and affection for others. She was not worried over the growing affection she felt for her novice mistress. The friendship that united them was very pure and could only help them in their desire to love God above all else. Her relationships were well ordered since she loved God above any human being and she loved others through God's love.

She gave her daily actions to God, working without hurry to stay in the present moment. She refused nothing given to her. She learned to prefer whatever happened. In her focus on God's mercy, she offered her littleness and nothingness to God. Through the discipline of giving her all (her nothingness without the illusion of being anything), she practiced loving others without reserve. This quick way was a surrender "in faith" of all return on her affect. Her sacrifice was to take the same delight in the difficult nuns as in the winsome ones. We might even say it was a "way of affect," to give whatever she felt to God. She was tested with aridity, feeling nothing, but she continued to act "as if" all was a joy for her.[14] And she says of herself that indeed she was very happy in spite of much suffering. Her surrender gave way to gratitude. Profound peace characterizes her writings. There's nothing childlike about her words, they illustrate a mature, full-bodied love. Her Little Way seems to me to be an excellent example of Cassian's fourth renunciation: that of the self.[15]

Everything she did was a ritual rather than simply a function. When she served as sacristan, filling the ciborium with hosts was a priestly act, but it also was an expression of her apostolate of filling heaven with souls.[16] She painted, wrote poetry and prose, accomplishing each task without becoming absorbed only in it. Her goal was not to be successful by making a public impression. She felt that our work should not hinder our praying. Our time should be used consciously, but with a detached heart. If we discover new imperfections in ourselves, we do something about it. Disappointments only motivate us to strive. Love like a child, but fight like Joan of Arc.[17] God calls us all to holiness. If we are called to the Little Way, we should practice it without desiring ecstasies or warm consolations. The Little Way is an apophatic way, a way of faith. A great desire, for instance, to imitate Joan of Arc in order to obtain sanctity, is not necessary. We should desire not to do outstanding works but to be invisible. This is a practice of virtue so hidden that the left hand doesn't know what the right hand is doing. It requires us to renounce ourselves, honor others, and be of service. We must be detached from results, let go of our needs and considerations.

To be a servant or a slave, subject to the whims and wishes of another, reverses our tendency toward self-love. God becomes visible through others. We let ourselves be found, loved, and fashioned by God. He always loves us first. We are little, empty. The practice asks us to keep empty so we can receive. We respond by loving others ahead of ourselves. In this Little Way, we let ourselves be carried, empty-handed, devoid of all merit, absolutely embraced gratuitously. God's love for us we see "in faith" and we demonstrate our love for God in service toward and sacrifice for others. We please God rather than merit affection from others.

Thérèse wanted to be completely immersed in the fire of love and offer herself to merciful love. She saw herself as a "victim, even a holocaust," consumed by the fire of Divine Love. This desire was a testimony that her deepest happiness was in being tested and found faithful. She did not see annihilation as a goal. Her goal was full immersion in and merging with Divine Love. Though she is sometimes perceived as childlike, she fully embraced suffering. Feminine in tone, she preferred the path of accepting the ordinary rather than the path of miracles, visions, and heroic mortifications.

We are attracted to the Little Way because this path helps us to recognize our nothingness, to expect everything from God, as a child expects everything from its father. We feel incapable of earning eternal life. St. Thérèse shows us however, that, like a child, we should simply pick flowers, the flowers of love and sacrifice, and offer them to God for his pleasure, doing very little things with great love.[18]

When we pray, as we practice the Little Way, we think about God, we free-associate, renouncing all that is not God. The path is one of faith, dark faith, with no content except faith. We join Jesus in the Gospels. Experiencing aridity, nothingness, no thought and no return on our efforts is to be expected. Prayers, reading, and devotions are difficult if not impossible at this stage.

For Thérèse, prayer was a movement of the heart, a simple gaze toward heaven, a cry of gratitude and love in the midst of trial as well as joy. However, she did not recite prayers in common without devotion. On the contrary, she loved common prayer because Jesus promised to be in the midst of those who gather in his name. Sometimes, if she could not concentrate on the mysteries of the rosary, she wrote them down or prayed the Hail Mary very slowly. Prayer was not easy for her, but it was essential.

Once she renounced deep silence during a retreat to talk to Sister Martha who was hurting. St. Thérèse's confession of the break in silence helped put her tendency toward scrupulosity behind her.[19] She never looked back after that confession.

Flowers were an idiom for her for how she saw beauty in the various things, events, and people in her path. Each thing was used for good, for beauty. St. Thérèse chose all and did all for God. Nothing was wasted. Nothing was too small. The "little" in her "Little Way" meant that everything is a means. Nothing is omitted and all is done in love. Her asceticism was rigorous and amazing in its totality and comprehensiveness; her aim was to be empty so that God is all. She allowed no escape for herself. She took no vacations from this ascetic path.

Her faith attracted her to the image of the Sacred Heart. Rather than seeing a picture of a man with an exposed heart, she saw John resting on

Jesus' bosom. She thought of her spouse's heart to be hers alone. She spoke to him in the solitude of his delightful heart, a heart-to-heart exchange, waiting for the day when she would contemplate him face to face. Another image of herself was the child climbing onto Jesus' lap and innocently hugging him.[20]

God calls all of us to holiness. We learn from St. Thérèse that the Little Way is without ecstasies or the consolation of spiritual presence. It is hidden. She let God be God, allowing God to find her, love her, fashion her. She never thought of herself as holy and wrote her story only under obedience. Her practice was laying aside anything for herself in her emotional life of feelings. She suffered willingly and offered her well-being as a sacrifice for the well-being of others.

The Practice of Self-Abandonment
of Jean-Pierre de Caussade

Jean-Pierre de Caussade was born in 1675 in southern France near Toulouse. In 1693 he became a Jesuit novice in Toulouse. He was ordained a priest in 1705 and received a doctorate in theology in 1715. De Caussade was given teaching posts until 1720 when he was assigned to the pastoral work of preaching missions. In 1730 he was sent to Nancy in Lorraine and directed a house of Visitation nuns. A year later he was assigned to a seminary, but in 1733 he returned to Nancy for six years. It was during this time that de Caussade's ministry of spiritual direction and his teaching of abandonment unfolded. He left Nancy for the last time in 1739 to serve as rector of two Jesuit houses. De Caussade's love of solitude and silence made such administrative duties taxing, but letters written to the Visitation nuns describe his willingness to abandon himself to each day's events as manifestations of God's will. The work known as Abandonment to Divine Providence *is a collection of his spiritual letters and conferences which was circulated privately by the Visitation nuns after his death in 1751 at the age of seventy-six. Another version of this work is entitled* The Sacrament of the Present Moment.

The essence of the teaching of de Caussade is that, since God is present in this moment and I can see only the present, I need to forget the past and not care about the future. Past thinking, he says, leads to discouragement and future thinking leads to anxiety and fear. Surrendering one's will to do the duty and necessity of the present moment leads us to abandon ourselves to God.

If I am looking for God's will, do I need to look at my life now? Yes, because my state in life, my vocation, is God's will. I can trust that this is so because in each previous moment I accepted the necessity of that moment. De Caussade goes on to say that nothing is small or trivial in God's eyes. This moment itself holds the will of God for me.

This would be a risky statement unless we presume we are leading a moral life. Confession is a natural beginning because all conscious sin committed in our former way of life is now forgiven and absolved. From that moment on, we can practice abandoning ourselves to God in the present moment, trusting in this practice because God is embodied in the present moment.

If God is in the present moment, we can therefore trust that God is manifest in our duty in that moment. We participate in God through fidelity to that duty. This is a profound teaching because duty is both passive and active. It is passive if we commit ourselves to do only what comes from the impulse of the Holy Spirit. But it is active when we carry that duty out. We don't do anything except what the impulse of the Holy Spirit dictates; we do only what we understand to be our duty in this instant.

The "one thing necessary" is always to be found by the soul in the present moment. There is no need to choose between prayer and silence, privacy or conversation, reading or writing, reflection or the abandonment of thought, the frequentation or avoidance of spiritual people, abundance or famine, illness or health, life or death; the "one thing necessary" is what each moment produces by God's design. "In this consists the stripping, the self-abnegation, the renunciation of the creature in order to be nothing by or for oneself, in order to remain as regards everything in God's order at his pleasure, finding one's only contentment in bearing the present moment, as if there were nothing else in the world to expect."[21]

This practice shifts our experience of God. At first we are in touch with God and God's impulses when we do this or that action. Then the shift takes place. We sense God acting through us, extending his presence through our actions of ordinary duty. This is a profound distinction. Let me try to present it for your consideration.

If we act "in God," apostolic acts are required, a rule of life is pre-scribed, direction is provided, we do what we do "for" God, we abandon ourselves. It's hard work. When the shift takes place and we experience "God in us," we are like a clay pot with no uses, broken, in the corner. Being present to God with full attention is the practice of doing God's will moment by moment, surrendering wholeheartedly any concern about the fruits of our action, placing ourselves in God's hands with no inner com-mentary about what we did and how what we did will be of benefit to our-selves or others.

In both levels of abandonment, we disengage the intellect and affect so that we attend to the "doing" of duty. Prayer isn't a conversation or a mantra; it is "no-thought," a selfless acting in faith. All will be well if we abandon ourselves to God. The abandonment is the prayer.

Our part is to be present to the moment, mindful; the present moment is offered to everyone.

This wonderful practice, abandonment to the present moment, avoids the problems of quietism since we take responsibility for right effort and for performing our duty according to the prompting of the Holy Spirit moment by moment. This practice of abandonment also avoids the dis-tinctions of other prayer practices. It doesn't matter whether we prefer devotional meditation or imageless prayer or contemplation. The present moment is the guide.

In the text, de Caussade writes with style and grace, repeating his rec-ommendations many times. Refrain from thoughts of the past or the future because the practice is to have faith in the present moment, to see God's signs in the present moment. At this moment we see the hand of God and we submit to God's will rather than to our own will. We reduce our curios-ity; we see less and believe more. We practice faith.

We measure our results by abandonment and surrender rather than by other outcomes. We humbly let God judge us. We expect mystery and lim-itations. It would be against the spirit and practice of this method to grumble or complain or show non-verbal resistance, either exteriorly or interiorly. We refrain from inner murmuring.

The present moment delights us. We see it as an opportunity for grace and mystery. It is our source of holiness.

The practice gains in intensity and we begin to anticipate surrender and to receive opportunities to surrender wholeheartedly. We practice docility and accept change willingly. We ask no questions about God's design for us.

The primary test of this practice is whether we can accept humiliations as part of the path. We disregard our natural resistance and our apparent opposition to the demands of the present moment and instead are confident in God's grace. We know this grace follows our willingness to undergo difficulties. Our job is to attend to the "now" in which we do our duty.

When we are on this path, we prefer to be hidden and ordinary since anonymity helps us replace self with faith. There is freedom here and low stress as we learn to do only what is inspired by the impulse of grace: no more and no less. All ambitions are ruled off the agenda. God's will—no more, no less.

There's also no need to discern one's state in life: duty names our vocation. Doing the present moment is more salvific than moving toward "higher" states in life. We bring our will, our intellect, and our imagination together to the single point of the present moment and this one-pointedness leads us to purity of heart.

We don't become deadened with this practice. We are alert to change because each moment contains the Holy Spirit's guidance. Because we practice docility, suppleness and readiness are our abiding dispositions.

In summary, we do our part and leave the rest to God. Having one thing or one thought at a time (reverently) in this moment is God. We abandon ourselves and receive God.

Positive Prayer Tools (Kataphatic)

THE PRACTICE OF THE PRESENCE OF GOD
OF BROTHER LAWRENCE

Brother Lawrence was born Nicholas Herman in 1611 in the Province of Lorraine, France. After military service, he became a footman in the service of the Treasurer of France. Wanting to give his life to God, he first became a hermit. This he found too depressing. In his late thirties he joined the Carmelites in Paris and was assigned kitchen duty. He found formal prayer tedious but discovered the Practice of the Presence while he did manual labor. Teaching this practice became his mission. He taught it to all who came to the kitchen or to his shoe shop. We have fourteen of his letters as well as his funeral eulogy and maxims that were collected by those who were taught by him. He died at age eighty-four. This Practice of the Presence is now taught in Hindu ashrams to those seeking to have their own experience of God.

What is practice of the presence? It is a vivid recollection of God's presence in the imagination or understanding. There are several descriptions: simple action, clear and distinct knowledge, an indistinct general gaze at God, remembrance of God, attention to God, silent conversation with God. The practice is actually "of faith," rather than of thinking "about God." The practice is neither meditation nor study. Work becomes worship. The emphasis is on faith and not much "on God." The presumed fact is that we believe that God is and is present.

How is the practice done? We choose frequently to recall the presence of God. This is called the practice of active presence. We live "as if" there were only God and ourselves in the world. We converse with God no matter where we go, asking God for what we need, unceasingly delighting God with total attention to the details of life. It is a sustained conversation.

If this sounds too good to be true, it does require much faith and sustained effort. We repeat this act of faith until it penetrates the depth of our soul. Over time we enter into heart-to-heart communication with God. We are gifted with his presence and communion happens. Outside events now never disturb the real peace we experience. A gentle loving gaze becomes our way of living and God lights the fire of our heart.

Brother Lawrence teaches that the soul only needs to consent. Our soul speaks to its deepest soul, the Holy Spirit. This practice of the presence moves from practice to a way of living. We experience nourishment in our soul. Instead of the soul doing a practice in the midst of its ordinary life, ordinary life becomes the practice. God expands our consciousness and we see God everywhere, in everyone and in everything, including ourselves.

While Brother Lawrence spent his days in the kitchen or as a shoe cobbler, he considered that his main work was "to remain in the presence of God with all the humility of an unprofitable, but nonetheless faithful servant."[22] To all who came to the back door he'd expound on this practice. He'd encourage them to start now no matter what troubles they were having in prayer or in living. He said, "When sinful, ask for mercy."

Notice he didn't say, if sinful, but when sinful. He had a profound sense of his own past and said of himself that he did not need a spiritual director, but a confessor! But he also said that, while it's not surprising how at risk all of us are, the good news is that we can still remain faithful without worry. He said we should replace worry with practice. Stop for a short moment, stop whatever you are doing as often as you can, and moment by moment adore God deep within your heart. Delight in him in secret. Nothing can stop you from practicing your faith. Talk to God. Notice God. Gaze at God. Shift your attention from your thoughts to your faith in God. "A multitude of thoughts crowd in on us and spoil everything."[23] Evil begins in our thoughts, so we must be careful to lay them aside as soon as we become aware that they are not essential to our present duties or to our salvation. Doing this allows us to begin our conversation with God once again.

For Brother Lawrence, this practice wasn't just for kitchen duty. His teaching is to remember God at prayer, because just being at prayer isn't prayer.

This practice of the presence is similar to but not the same as colloquy. As the impulse to remember the presence comes, we should lift it to prayer in colloquy. Presence is spontaneous; colloquy is a steady effort to shift all self-talk to God rather than have inner talk only to the self.

Brother Lawrence fine-tuned the French preference for the "practice of simple regard." This momentary glance of simple regard is noticing God looking at me! He recommends using our own words in our conversation with God, letting whatever comes to our mind be the response: Lord, bless my work![24]

This kind of practice doesn't need a cell, a shrine, or a sanctuary. We make our hearts a prayer room into which we retire from time to time to converse with him gently, humbly, and lovingly. "One way to call your mind easily back to God during your fixed prayer times and to hold it more steady is not to let it take much flight during the day. You must keep it strictly in the presence of God."[25] As we become used to doing this over and over, it is easier to remain at peace during our prayer times, or at least to recall our mind from its wanderings.

With God, we talk about whatever is on our minds. We ask for grace, offer sufferings. During conversation with others we lift our heart toward God from time to time; the slightest little remembrance, Brother Lawrence says, will always be very pleasant to God.

The practice of the presence is not so much about a conversation as it is about an act of living faith. We talk to God as if God's here. Most of the time we act as if God is not here. This is a reversal and a change of heart that has immense consequences for our interior life.

There are many benefits to this practice. We ask for help and then overcome temptations. We lead a life closer to our desire for God. If God grants our desire, we have a felt presence of God that may last for days, weeks, or years. This presence kindles love. Our desire becomes more sharply focused. We try to live and live only in the presence of God. And for some rare souls the practice of the presence accompanies them through the sufferings of this life and even through the stages of dying.

The practice of simple regard sometimes shows itself not in a thought of God, but of pain. This pain can be a prayer. Brother Lawrence teaches how suffering that is used like a prayer can become redemptive.[26] He assures the one suffering that God's work on their behalf is being accomplished through their time of trial. He is direct in telling them not to waste all their time on seeking remedies for their suffering, but in surrendering to God's way for them. He also assures them of his prayers. [27]

The Practice of Colloquy of Gabrielle Bossis

There are many saints in the Christian tradition who have a transcendent experience of God breaking into their ordinary consciousness. Some report raptures, wounds of love, visions, and locutions. None of those epic events describe the practice of colloquy, as I understand it.

One such saint who used colloquy at the invitation of Our Lord was Gabrielle Bossis born in Nantes in 1874, the youngest of four children.

Gabrielle had a degree in nursing but her life work was writing, producing, and acting in entertaining comedies and morally pointed dramas. She was invited to many countries including Canada and most of Europe. She resisted pressure to join a convent but found her vocation using her talents in the arts in the world. She also resisted marriage but did not resist being a wealthy woman with fine things in good taste. On rare occasions she was surprised by Christ's voice, but from age sixty-two until she died on June 9th, 1950 at age seventy-six she had an ongoing dialogue with Our Lord. He directed her to write a journal and in this hidden double life we learn that she led an extroverted life of acting and being a celebrity and then wrote at Our Lord's direction fragments of her conversations with God that were compiled into He and I, *first published in France.*[28]

A mark of authenticity in this book is that the entries are all about Christ's words to Gabrielle. We learn very little about Gabrielle. She is merely an instrument. What has attracted me to this book, over and over again, is how Our Lord invites and coaches Gabrielle to speak, think, and be with him. It's a teaching which leads directly into Christ consciousness. There are other books about Christ consciousness but no better instruction that is available to each of us should we respond to the invitation.

The first moment is an event that happens to many of us. We awaken to the real presence of Jesus. Then we participate in that presence by sharing our thoughts with him. We listen "as if" we hear him, "as if" through our imagination comes a "voice." At that moment we don't consider ourselves in a "for-real" conversation. But we are in a "for-real" practice of faith.

The practice of colloquy is to shift the "I-thoughts" to thought of sharing "in faith" with Jesus. Self-talk at first might seem like auto-suggestion, but as we see it unfolding in *He and I*, it becomes communion. Our prayer becomes a sharing of all our waking thoughts. Our desires are directed to him. If we are attracted to using an image of the Sacred Heart or the Good Shepherd or Jesus walking to Emmaus in our colloquy, soon our experience of that prayer becomes adoration. We remain in the presence, sometimes sharing thoughts, at other times in total silence with only a loving gaze. This is no one-hour-a-day event. Our daily life is accompanied by this inner dialogue with Jesus. Everything is shared. (Notice we don't bring Jesus to our daily life in intercessory prayer, our daily life *is* the prayer.) All our "work" is done both really and symbolically for Jesus, in the presence of Jesus.

"Don't fail to supernaturalize everything, night and day. It is My life that is living in you now, not yours. Adore. Give thanks. And when I ask you to be simple, I mean above all in your relations with Me. Don't get the idea that I need any special words or gestures; just be yourself. Who is closer to you than God?"[29]

The practice requires us to take each impulse of grace and follow it consciously and conscientiously toward God in love. While Gabrielle didn't care about stages of relationship, we can witness how her relationship with Jesus evolved from an acquaintance to a dear friend, and how her commitment finally merged into union.

It is interesting to note that Gabrielle accepted suffering as a test of strength, of how firm she was in her resolve. She turned toward the path of selflessness and suffering, shifting the feelings of her heart toward Our Lord and his suffering for us. Sacrifice became part of the exchange.

This practice trains the will. Her consent was to notice the subtle requests asked for in each impulse of grace. Her "willingness" was to do the will of the Beloved. She strove to focus her attention on imitating Jesus, following his directives, focusing on his love and her loving him in return. Intimacy abounded.

Imitation in her life, as in ours, gives way to co-creating with Our Lord: doing work on behalf of others. This work ranges from little acts of kindness to picking up others' suffering. Intercessory prayer is dynamic and productive.

We see that her outward work, or apostolic service, was only to do God's will (not to get anything done). For Gabrielle work as an artist was real, insofar as she did much good, but it was primarily a medium to give form to her relationship with Our Lord.

She was vigilant never to believe that she had made it. She had a profound sense of otherness and separation from God. She saw herself as sinner. She practiced guard of the heart continuously so as to be worthy of this inner dialogue with the Savior. When she failed in some way, she simply and humbly named the act and asked for forgiveness. She did not waste time on her own feelings of guilt, desiring only Our Lord's intimacy.

This intimacy was mediated through signs, like birds and sunsets. She received them as flowers from the beloved. Her rich exchange with Jesus was normal and everyday, as lovers are wont to have. In a charming exchange with Gabrielle, Jesus says, "Talk to Me, for Me there is no sweeter prayer."[30]

We see signs of *lectio*, of her entering the Lord's life as depicted in the Gospels. The title *He and I* is somewhat misleading because there's no hint of domesticating Jesus to fit her personal agenda. The Christ consciousness that emerges in Gabrielle is of a soul who inspires all of us.[31] Through her love of Our Lord, she transformed her life in order to participate in the redemption of all humankind.

The path of colloquy is one of love, surrender, humility, and devotion. Often persons attracted to colloquy use music, song, affective melodies, chants, and ceaseless repetition of the name of the Beloved. We have a specific image of Our Lord and give our total attention to Christ, our teacher, friend, and spouse, Our Beloved. Self-talk is silent when union abides. Sacrifice replaces self-interest. Union happens when there's no agenda.

THE PRACTICE OF RECOLLECTION OF ST. TERESA OF AVILA

Sister Teresa of Jesus was born Teresa de Cepeda y Humada in 1515 to a wealthy family in Avila, Spain. Beautiful, charming, and outgoing, she entered the local Carmelite convent in 1536. For some twenty years she struggled with serious illness and the somewhat lax religious life of her convent. Her spiritual fervor faded and for a year she even abandoned prayer altogether. In 1554 she experienced a "reconversion" after seeing a statue of the wounded Christ. With renewed ardor Teresa eventually regained her spiritual equilibrium and emerged to conduct the reform of her Carmelite order. In 1562 she founded St. Joseph's Convent in Avila, the first convent of the Carmelite reform. A tireless worker, she founded twenty more convents before her death in 1582 at the age of sixty-seven. Teresa's extraordinary insight into the process of spiritual growth has been transmitted through her writing. The Life *is an autobiographical work which tells of her own spiri-*

tual development up to the point when she founded her first convent. Works which present her spiritual teachings are The Way of Perfection, *written for the sisters of St. Joseph's Convent, and* The Interior Castle, *her most thorough and orderly description of the spiritual life.*

Recollection is a practice recommended by St. Teresa of Avila. She speaks of active and passive recollection. Right effort for active recollection is to gather in our senses and lift up our mind to God. She says, "I tell you that for wandering minds it is very important not only to believe these truths but to strive to understand them by experience."[32] And she goes on to say, "What I'm trying to point out is that we should see and be present to the One with whom we speak without turning our backs on Him, for I don't think speaking with God while thinking of a thousand other vanities would amount to anything else but turning our backs on Him."[33]

She understood that harm comes from not truly understanding that God is near, but instead imagining him as far away. St. Teresa had immediacy with God as an abiding consciousness. We should live "in faith" and look at God in our attention. Since indeed how far away is God? Should we go to the heaven to seek him! No, God's face is here. Should we not look at it when it is so close to us? In common face-to-face dialogue is it rude not to look at the one speaking? So, the first step of the practice of recollection is to think of God as near rather than far away. This is our faith.

Teresa taught that we have heaven within us since the Lord of heaven is here within our earthly mind's eye. We only need to recollect ourselves. We need to listen to what we are saying in our prayers and listen to the one to whom we are speaking. To do this we need to be attentive. Our exterior senses must be recollected. The senses need to be occupied. She offers a distinct method to do this training of the mind.

First, we must slow down our thoughts, think of God, and focus our attention on God rather than review our thoughts or turn over concepts in our mind. One way of slowing down the mind is recollection. God is within. All one needs to do is go into solitude, look within, and not turn away from so good a guest, but with great humility speak to God as to a father. Beseech him; tell him about your trials; ask him for a remedy against them, realizing that you are not worthy to be his daughter. The Lord is within us and it is there that we must be with him.³⁴ The practice here is to turn our mind's eye toward Our Lord, to tune into the presence within us.

We must leave aside any faintheartedness that refuses Our Lord's invitations. St. Teresa tells us to take God at his word. "Since He is your Spouse, He will treat you accordingly."³⁵ She teaches that at the moment of recollection the divine Master comes more quickly to teach the soul and give it the prayer of quiet than he does through any other method. "This prayer is called 'recollection,' because the soul collects its faculties together and enters within itself to be with its God. And its divine Master comes more quickly to teach it and give it the prayer of quiet than He would through any other method it might use."³⁶ Even though passive recollection may happen later in our practice, we will always need to return to active recollection from time to time. There's no one who is not a beginner.

In recollection we keep our eyes closed often as we pray. We strive not to look at things. This striving is necessary at the beginning; afterward, there is no need to strive, the greater effort then is to open the eyes while praying. Later, it is difficult not to keep praying after the time for prayer bids us to attend to other activities.

St. Teresa cautions the practitioner about heavy seas. It seems the soul is aware of being strengthened and fortified in recollection at the expense of the body, leaving the body alone and weakened. But the soul receives in this recollection a supply of provisions to strengthen it against the body's tendency to demand attention and the mind's tendency to be scattered. Recollection is a withdrawing of the senses from exterior things and a renunciation of them in such a way that our thoughts are not attracted to them. The eyes close so as to avoid seeing them and so that the sight may be more awake to the things of the soul. There's no need to think holy thoughts. God doesn't need them and often they take us into vainglory. So, recollection in and of itself is prayer. She goes on to teach her sisters that the important thing is not to think much but to love much; and so do that which best stirs you to love.³⁷

There are, however, greater and lesser degrees of recollection. In the beginning the body causes us difficulties because it claims its rights without realizing that it is cutting off its own head by not surrendering. But if we make the effort and practice this recollection for some days, we will clearly see the gain. We will begin to understand, when we start to pray, that the bees are approaching and entering the beehive to make honey. And recollection will be effected without effort because the Lord has desired that, during the time the faculties are drawn inward, the soul will dominate. Eventually when the soul does no more than give a sign that it wishes to be recollected, the senses obey and become recollected.[38]

Even though the senses go out again afterward, their having already surrendered is a great thing; for they go out as captives and subjects that do not cause harm as they did previously. And when the will calls them back again, they come more quickly, until after many of these entries the Lord wills that they rest entirely in perfect contemplation.

When we get used to the practice of recollection, because there is no impediment from outside, the soul enjoys being alone with God. Eventually you can't recollect yourself by force but only by gentleness, if your recollection is going to be more continual.[39] Since the soul is close to the fire, a little spark will ignite and set everything ablaze.

We must disengage ourselves from everything so as to approach God interiorly, and even in the midst of occupations withdraw within ourselves. "Although it may be for only a moment that I remember I have that Company within myself, doing so is very beneficial. In sum, we must get used to delighting in the fact that it isn't necessary to shout in order to speak to Him, for His Majesty will give the experience that He is present."[40]

Recollection is not something supernatural given to a few special souls; it is something we can desire and learn ourselves—though always with the help of God, for without this help we can do nothing, not even have good thoughts. To expect it to just happen is not realistic. We must work to build our relationship with God. Recollection is not a silence of the faculties; it is an enclosure of the faculties within the soul. The practice of recollection is a manner of praying that the soul gets so quickly used to that it doesn't go astray, nor do the faculties become restless, as time shows us. Teresa says, "I only ask that you try this method, even though it may mean some struggle; everything involves struggle before the habit is acquired. But I assure you that before long it will be a great consolation for you to know that you can find this holy Father, whom you are beseeching, within you without tiring yourself in seeking where He is."[41]

Recollection lies within our power. It involves a gradual increase of self-control and an end to vain wandering from the right path; it means conquering, making use of one's senses for the sake of the inner life. If you speak, strive to remember that the one with whom you are speaking is present within you. If you listen, remember that you are going to hear one who is very close to you when he speaks. In sum, bear in mind that you can, if you want, avoid ever withdrawing from such good company; and be sorry that for a long time you left your Father alone, of whom you are so much in need.

She goes on to recommend: "If you can, practice this recollection often during the day; if not, do so a few times. As you become accustomed to it you will experience the benefit, either sooner, or later. Once this recollection is given by the Lord, you will not exchange it for any treasure. Since nothing is learned without a little effort, consider, Sisters, for the love of God, as well employed the attention you give to this method of prayer. I know, if you try, that within a year, or perhaps half a year, you will acquire it, by the favor of God. See how little time it takes for a gain as great as is that of laying a good foundation."[42]

These teachings are from *The Way of Perfection*. In her systematic work, *The Interior Castle*, she moves from active recollection to passive recollection, depending upon which mansion the soul is dwelling in. Here's a short summary of her teachings in *The Interior Castle* pertaining to recollection. In that book, St. Teresa speaks of a gradual immersion into God and God into us. The castle is entered into by prayer. Prayer is the doorway that opens up into the mystery of God.[43] In the first dwellings, effort starts slowly as desire for God begins to supplant all previous desires.

In the first dwelling, the seeker says prayers but is still distracted and involved in worldly things such as possessions, honor, or business affairs. She prays only on occasion.[44]

In the second dwelling, the seeker begins to practice prayer and notices the prompting and invitation of Christ's grace that comes from external sources like books, sermons, friendships, and trials. The goal of one's striving is conformity with God's will.[45]

In the third dwelling, the seeker recognizes the desire to have her own experience of God. She begins ascetical practices to remove obstacles and starts to practice periods of recollection. She uses her time well, reaches out toward neighbors, and conforms her external life to her interior desires. She fears consequences to her health and has much difficulty parting with wealth. She is shocked by the faults of others and quickly distraught by a little dryness. She needs someone who is free of the world's illusions with whom she might speak.[46]

Between the third and fourth dwellings, there is a shift in the practice of recollection. In the fourth dwelling, the supernatural begins. Infused prayer happens. The soul learns that it's important not to think much but to love much. Right effort is to please God in everything, to strive, insofar as possible, not to offend him and to ask him for the advancement of the honor and glory of his Son. This contemplative prayer begins with a passive experience of recollection, a gentle drawing of the faculties inward; it is different from recollection achieved at the cost of human effort. This prayer of infused recollection is a less intense form of initial contemplation or, as called by Teresa, the prayer of quiet. While the will finds rest in the prayer of quiet, in the peace of God's presence, the intellect (in Teresa's terminology) continues to move about. Distractions, a wandering mind, are a part of the human condition and can no more be avoided than can eating and sleeping. To grow in this prayer, one must let the intellect go and surrender oneself into the arms of love.[47]

In describing the fifth dwelling, she speaks of the prayer of union wherein the faculties become completely silent. The soul has a certitude that it is in God and God is in it. At times the soul is dead to itself and completely free. She uses a marriage symbolism: the soul and Our Lord become engaged . . . getting to know one another. The soul's effort is to attend to humility and service to others.[48]

In the sixth dwelling, she moves the marriage symbolism toward betrothal. She speaks of courage to endure trials both exterior and interior, of severe illnesses, of inner sufferings, fears, and misunderstanding on the part of the confessor and consequent anxiety that God will allow one to be deceived, and of a feeling of unbearable inner oppression and even of being rejected by God. The sixth dwelling is characterized by spiritual awakenings and deep impulses. The woundings of love cause both pain and delight. The betrothal takes place when "His Majesty gives the soul raptures that draw it out of its senses. For if it were to see itself so near this great majesty while in its senses, it would perhaps die."[49] Though the soul in ecstasy is without consciousness in its outward life, it was never before so awake to the things of God, nor did it ever before have so deep an enlightenment and knowledge of God. Illuminations teach the soul.

She explains the distinction between discursive meditation about Christ and contemplative presence with him. The inability of contemplative souls to engage in discursive thought about the mysteries of the passion and life of Christ in their prayer is very common. But contemplating these mysteries, dwelling in them with a simple gaze, will not impede the most sublime prayer. She insists on staying in contact with Christ's humanity and divinity. It's important that the contemplative enter into union with her body/mind/soul and not transcend the body. Failure to do this stops the soul's progress into the last two dwelling places.

There are no closed doors between the sixth and seventh dwellings. The unity of the soul is natural. This is a place in the extreme interior, a place very deep within itself. The grace of a spiritual marriage, of perfect union, is bestowed. The goal of the spiritual journey is union with Christ, now no longer living as the divine Logos but as the resurrected Word Incarnate. The fruit of this marriage is good works. An interior calm fortifies these persons so that, even though they may endure much stress in the exterior events of their lives, they may have the strength to serve.

Works of service may be outstanding ones, but they need not be. One must concentrate on serving those who are in one's company. The Lord doesn't look so much at the greatness of our works as at the love with which they are done. His Majesty will join our sacrifice with that which he offered for us.[50] "Thus even though our works are small they will have the value our love for Him would have merited had they been great."[51]

The practice of recollection accompanies the practitioner, but a good sign is to reduce words, mental work, and involvement of the imagination. A spiritual director can assist with discernment. At first it is important to have someone who has experience of recollection and discretion in judgment. Later when there's experience of the mansions it would be good to have a learned person who can detect truth and deliver us from foolish devotions that keep us at a superficial level. Reading spiritual classics is a great advantage in assisting us with recollection, in centering our thoughts, but also in raising up truth to match our experience.

Biblical Practices

THE PRACTICE OF GRACED SUFFERING

Each of the methods we have considered includes the theme of suffering. By way of emphasis I'd like to point out that a sign of integration of any practice is how we deal with suffering. As Christians ours is the cross, not only confounding outsiders, or even our ecclesial communities, but also finding its way into each one of our lives. We know there is no escape from suffering.

We learn from those who have gone before us that suffering can be accepted and transmuted into a benefit. This is a most difficult path. Since we all suffer it seems that we are all called to it. If we look into the Christian Scriptures we find that Jesus himself laid down his life not only at the time of death but in his humble birth, years of teaching, healing and preaching. Not only did he personally suffer but he suffered with those burdened with afflictions.

If we look at the letters of St. Paul and St. Peter we can know that suffering is an actual path that we can follow and be comforted that while "suffering is at work" in us we can be saved. We start with a humble disposition of having the same mind as Jesus (Phil. 2:5–11). Christ emptied himself and we are to empty ourselves likewise.

This need not be sad and done because there is no other door to the next life. We actually continue the work of Christ through our suffering in our particular time, place, and circumstances. Our participation in suffering actually continues Christ Jesus' work of salvation and transfiguration. Graced suffering is an extension of the mystery of the incarnation (Col. 1:24).

Indeed, we derive consolation when we know that our suffering has a public dimension and is a service to others (2 Cor. 1:3–7). It's not the theory of suffering or the fact of it, but my own suffering that makes a difference for others and our fragile planet. In fact, it is our very weakness that is the tool to participate in Christ's redemptive work (2 Cor. 4:7–12).

Graced suffering is the human side of the paschal mystery (1 Pet. 2:21–25). We can embrace our suffering with the assurance that suffering has intelligibility despite its physical and emotional pain because God's love gives it meaning. Again, our experience of weakness and a subtle strength to stay the course with a loving heart gives teeth to the scriptural testimonies. We can walk in faith without a felt experience of the Presence. This is our hope that is living, conscious, and active (Rom. 5:1–5). We actually receive the power of Christ in this grace-filled event (2 Cor. 12:7b–10).

This paradox of when I'm weak, I'm actually strong is a sense of life and well-being while dying. Here at the monastery we often witness a healthy sister who happens to be dying. It's a joy to behold. She passes, we remain faithful. Last month we buried Sister Mary Edwin. Her death was about a nine month process, but the suffering was certainly a journey to and toward her heart's desire. We kept vigil with her. The entire house was grace with joy-filled peace (Phil. 37–11).

We are all called to relieve the burden of the poor. We must heal the sick and be part of the solution to such problems as the uneven distribution of food on our planet, or violence, or oppression. The Christian mandate is to love, to serve, and to extend the healing touch of Christ to others without regard for who they are. In fact, we are called to honor our enemies, supporting and lovingly anticipating their needs.

For ourselves, after we've made the right effort to live a healthy, balanced, and wholesome life, we must accept afflictions whether of body, mind, or soul.

If we were to take up the practice of suffering, it would look like this: we would lay aside our fear of being sick or harmed. If that happens, it is simply an event that can be an opportunity for good. We'd look for ways of healing, but after reasonable effort we'd accept the necessity of our being mortal. We would bring to prayer our feelings, thoughts and discomforts of body/mind/soul. We'd pray for the grace to receive God's will. This prayer might ask for deliverance, for perseverance, or even for letting the disease take our life and transform us in death as we accept the consequences of entering the next life. This prayer may or may not be answered in a way we can discern, but we would continue "in faith" to accept whatever is. For our salvation we'd practice faith again and again as we feel the pain, the fear, the anxiety, the discomfort, and the confusion.

The next phase would be to shift our pain-thought to God and lift the very pain-thought as prayer. We would do this as many times as the thought comes to mind and let the pain do the work of prayer. The practice is prayer; the medium is pain. All the suffering involved with the pain is also prayer. We notice the discomfort of others, the concern of the caregivers, the expense of the treatment, the loss of work, and maybe even the demise of relationships, dreams, hopes, and ambitions. It is not just our body that undergoes death. We let the pain be lifted up and we do not attempt any other kind of prayer; accepting the suffering in faith is our prayer.

If we suffer the illness only for a short time, our effort would be to let the pain purify our intentions, our previous way of life, the misguided or unreconciled events of our past. We let the pain absorb those vicissitudes into a new way of doing only the will of God.

The grace of "suffering for" is to let my suffering be of benefit for others. Can the benefit of my pain, united with Christ's suffering on the cross, be transferred to another who is in need of loving mercy? If this grace is granted, my suffering is a gift to someone else.

There is mystery in suffering. No conceptual answer is satisfying. However, from experience we know that suffering accomplishes more than any other method. It prompts conversion and heals layers of the soul that can't be touched by words, beauty, and friendship. We know that suffering has a purpose and is not to be wasted. There is urgency about suffering. Both in being born to this life as we emerge from our mothers and in being born into eternal life on our deathbed we witness the power of suffering. Some suffering subsides for a time, some pain returns in this lifetime, but all suffering passes. It's our choice what to make of it! Suffering is difficult, but not without its particular grace. As Christians we follow the way of the cross to the resurrection.

THE PAULINE PRACTICE OF
NO PREFERENCE

This practice came out of the lived experience of a nun here at Our Lady of Grace Monastery. She discovered that St. Paul taught and lived a practice that she had discovered through her own life. She writes this reflection using the Pauline Epistles for *lectio divina.*

About a year ago, in a time of "fear and trembling," I listened to a series of tapes, characterized as a rediscovery of life, by Anthony de Mello, S.J.; he was speaking about the path to true peace and happiness, to life. De Mello contended that the answer, the truth, was in all the main spiritual traditions, if only we could and would hear. For his purposes, he focused on the way the Buddhist tradition taught this truth: the world is full of sorrow, the root of sorrow is attachment (desire), the uprooting of sorrow is the dropping of attachment (desire).[52] However, he had begun with Paul's words in Philippians: "For I have learned, in whatever situation I find myself, to be self-sufficient. I know indeed how to live in humble circumstances; I know also how to live with abundance. In every circumstance and in all things I have learned the secret of being well fed and of going hungry, of living in abundance and of being in need" (Phil. 4:11–12). This, along with the Sermon on the Mount, was the Christian articulation of this truth, according to de Mello.[53] The tapes were transformative for me. I was struck with Paul's words. I wanted to find out for myself, did Paul speak of a non-attachment practice? If Paul was speaking of a non-attachment practice what was it rooted in, certainly not the Buddhist's "emptiness." I set out to answer this question for myself, not out of intellectual curiosity, but because the practice, which I rooted in Christ, had become a deep truth for me. I went to the letters of Paul, and found what I believe to be that practice, rooted in Christ.[54]

For Paul, now, with Christ, all is a new creation, infused with the Spirit of God, Christ. The only life, reality, power there is now is Christ, life in Christ, all else is finite, *maya,* illusion, non-reality, and there is still evil which is death. Those of this new creation have received life from God's Spirit, now working in them and in the world. They have been baptized into the only life there is, life in Christ. This life is a movement. It is as if a motor has been turned on and all life is in Christ, moving toward God. Therefore, if the only life is life in Christ, once one has chosen life, there can be no attachment to any person, state, or thing, no preference for a form of life, the content is all Christ. There is only Christ.

All is now a new creation for Paul, the only reality, the only life, is Christ, and we, by adoption, participate in it. "Consequently, from now on we regard no one according to the flesh; even if we once knew Christ according to the flesh, yet now we know him so no longer. So whoever is in Christ is a new creation: the old things have passed away; behold, new things have come. And all this is from God" (2 Cor. 5:16–18). "But may I never boast except in the cross of our Lord Jesus Christ, through which the world has been crucified to me, and I to the world. For neither does circumcision mean anything, not does uncircumcision, but only a new creation" (Gal. 6:14–15). "I have been crucified with Christ; yet I live, no longer I, but Christ lives in me" (Gal. 2:19b–20).

Christ's Spirit changed everything. All life is now Christ. This is life infused with the Spirit, and we have been called into that life, in Christ, in the Spirit of God. "But when the fullness of time had come, God sent his Son, born of a woman, born under the law, to ransom those under the law, so that we might receive adoption. As proof that you are his children, God sent the Spirit of his Son into our hearts, crying out, 'Abba, Father!'" (Gal. 4:4–6). "God is faithful, and by him you were called to fellowship with his Son, Jesus Christ our Lord" (1 Cor. 1:9). "But we have the mind of Christ" (1 Cor. 2:16b). We share Christ's life, and this life is a movement that is only Christ.

All life is Christ. If this is Paul's reality there can be no attachment to anything. There is only Christ; all else is illusion or death. Paul knows he belongs to Christ. He knows there is no life now, except life in Christ, in which he partakes. Therefore, he could not believe acquiring something he does not have, or holding on to something he could lose, would make him happy or content. He has no attachment. There is only Christ. Once again, ". . . for I have learned, in whatever situation I find myself, to be self-sufficient" (Phil. 4:11b). He will eat and enjoy food when it is there; he will go hungry when it is not. His worldly circumstances do not dictate his well-being, because the only real circumstance is Christ.

Hence, he also has no preference for any particular state of life. His only preference is God; so stay in the state of life you were living when God called you, because, then you are not asserting your preference, that is, will. If you are married stay married, if single, stay single, circumcised, uncircumcised, remain that way. "Only, everyone should live as the Lord has assigned, just as God called each one" (1 Cor. 7:17a). It appears that Paul realizes that to try to alter one's state in life could possibly be to exercise attachment. With non-attachment to thoughts of my preference, it is possible to see Christ and follow the impulse of grace. Paul does seem to recognize human weakness and account for it. Better to change one's state of life than sin. "If anyone thinks he is behaving improperly toward his virgin, and if a critical moment has come and so it has to be, let him do as he wishes. He is committing no sin; let them get married" (1 Cor. 7:36).

How this works as a practice is like this.[55] Awareness is the key. I accept and understand that life is Christ, God, and that I participate in this life, all else is illusion or death. Non-attachment is when I see myself desiring something, a person, thing, food, praise, power, and so forth; I think those thoughts and emotions through to see that there is nothing I lack, that I and others have been just fine, at other times, without whatever the particular object of focus is. Happiness and contentment are dependent on nothing; they are the facts of my existence, existence is Christ. I chose not to live in illusion and death. I chose not to live the lie. No attachment, only Christ. Purity of heart, single pointedness, is. I chose Christ at every moment, and the way that is done is by accepting all that is not sin/evil that comes one's way. I do not chase other things, because my eye is on Christ. Christ is reality and I exist in that reality. There is nothing real to chase. A note of caution with this practice: I must take care not to fall into the delusion that if I have no attachment, why not satisfy my desires, and live the life-style I desire. A wise elder would help discern.

For Paul all life is Christ. Christ is the only reality, and through the Spirit, we participate in that reality. To live in a state of attachment (desire), and to chase our desires, is to miss Christ, life. If we practice awareness so our thoughts do not rule us, we will experience life, Christ.

7

TOOLS OF DISCERNMENT

Discernment Is Sorting

To discern is to sort out, in the light of the whole, that which is of God. The goal of discerning is to reach purity of heart, a single point of light. Often we get caught up in a part, such as food or sex, and sometimes that single part becomes our god, or an idol. The ascetical practices used by the monastics in the desert were intended to reverse this tendency to make gods of our selves or our things or events rather than let God be God in our lives. As a result of original sin we find ourselves in a condition that requires discernment. We have a tendency toward evil. We are ignorant of the good, or our wills are weak even when we know what is good and attempt to strive against evil. This is our human condition, and means that the work of discernment helps us know what is good, how to avoid evil, and how to be strong in our resolve to take refuge in Christ.

We can rely on the elders' experience from the desert tradition. Their teachings about the eight thoughts contain teachings about discernment.

Here's a summary listing: we notice our thoughts. Usually a thought comes with a tail of little thoughts. If the first thought doesn't catch our attention, then the second or third one will. With the practice of watchfulness of thoughts, we can observe our thoughts and catch the moment we consent to the thought instead of letting it pass by. It's this consent that is our moment for choosing truth.

From the food-thought we learn that fasting is a natural way to notice thoughts because it is easy to sense hunger. We can practice noticing the hunger-thought, letting it pass by or consenting to it. When we learn this, we learn the first step in discernment: in order to take the middle way, moderation is preferred:

- Not too much, not too little.
- Not too often, not too infrequent.
- Not too rich in quality, not too poor in quality.
- Extremes meet. It is risky to be on the edges. It's not recommended to eat too little, as it is not recommended to eat too much.

From the sex-thought we learn that thoughts have a life of their own. We are not our thoughts, but we get hooked on them and they become a cycle. To break the cycle of thoughts, we should manifest them to a trusted elder. The disciple practices humility and the elder practices discernment and can often give a word to assist the discerning one.

We must not manifest our thoughts to just any older person. He or she should be beyond the afflictions themselves, at least beyond the predominant one that the disciple has trouble with. Even if there isn't an elder around, it is good to manifest thoughts, but the seeker is to disregard the example or advice of the elder if it is not in concert with the teachings from the desert tradition.

We must discern our sex-thoughts at the first inkling before they cluster into feelings or passions. If we notice them soon, we can frequently redirect them swiftly. The goal is prayer and the abiding sense of God's presence rather than consciousness of food, sex, things, anger, and so forth. We strive to be the same in the night as we are in the day.

From the thing-thought we see the value of refraining from analysis of thoughts except to sort through the source of the thought: self, God, or the devil. If the source is self, then appropriate remedies should be taken. If from God, then I need secure permission to use the things. If from evil, I must rid myself of the things and root out the attraction toward greed.

Things also need the same discerning moderation: how many is more than I need; how many is too few? Having things too high or too low in quality also violates the spirit of using things as tools to mediate God. Too much time used in managing things snuffs out the spiritual life. The illusion of personal ownership needs to be rooted out. We are all creatures using "things" as vessels of the altar.

From the anger-thought we see the harm done to our ability to discern if we are afflicted with anger. We cannot see ourselves and are of no help to others when we are angry. We are blind. We cannot discern when we are angry, so anger must be entirely rooted out. Forgiveness can even anticipate the potential of anger.

The dejection-thought teaches us to find the source of dejection. Is it from anger unresolved, harm done, dashed expectations, sin that fragments the mind and divides the heart, or is it chemical? Treatment depends on the cause. If from sin, confess. If depression is from unresolved anger, forgive. If it's from unknown origins, compassion. If the source is exaggerated self-esteem, then humility is the remedy.

From the acedia-thought we learn that we are not the best judge of ourselves. When we are bored and tempted to abandon the spiritual journey, we need to stay in our cells, return to the routine of the monastic life, and do manual labor. We need to cultivate compunction. We desire truth, which is humility. Work becomes prayer, and prayer and work are interchangeable.

From the vainglory-thought we learn how to discern whether we are being self-centered rather than selfless. We understand that we must refrain from daydreams and fantasy where we are the center of attention. We learn that our motivation (our thought about the thought) matters. We learn that we can do all the right things for the wrong reasons. Discernment helps us factor out our second thoughts, that is, our intentions. These must be sorted too: is our intention from God, from self-interest, or from evil inclinations? When motivations are true, the monastery can be the world and your cell is your heart.

From the pride-thought we learn the steps of humility: to align our thoughts, words, and deeds with truth. In pride we see the results of thoughts that have origins rooted in evil. If their source is from evil spirits, we need to be alert. Evil spirits do exist and to encourage persons to deny them is a weapon used by evil spirits (*Conf.* 8:12.1). Cassian says we have two spirits, one our guardian angel and the other a demon trying to snatch our souls (*Conf.* 8:17.1). Demons cannot read our thoughts but can see our outward demeanor and tempt us according to what they perceive as our weakness. There are many varieties of evil beings, some more harmful than others. Some are neutral. They seem to specialize in certain areas of concentration related to the eight afflictions.

Afflictions can have two sources: our own inner dispositions or evil spirits from without. We need to have a healthy regard for demons and their destructive power.[1] They have higher intelligence than humans and can enter our bodies and even our minds without our consent. While demons can disturb our minds with confusion and even possession, they cannot take over our souls unless we consent. This is why we must be vigilant and know ourselves, know when we consent and when we refuse temptation and cancel the attraction. Demons are of varying degrees of evil. Most of the time they do not seem evil but come in the form of light, either as a good that is not God, or an apparent good that wins our affections.

What do these embodied spirits look like? Demons are creatures with subtle bodies (not material ones) and with consciousness and intelligence. They come in differing forms for their dark work in the world. The Scriptures contain the names of animals given to a variety of devils to indicate the range of their cunning, haunting, attractive, repulsive, or magical appearances. Demons are both light and dark. Some come through doors, make noises, and incite negative feelings. Others are sweet, friendly; give counsel and the confidence to perform spiritual feats.

Demons are repelled by good. Sacramentals, for example, holy water, a crucifix, medals, and blessed candles, are forces against evil. The prayer taught by our Lord, the Our Father, has a depth and power equal to match any evil in our fragile world. Most evil forces are held in check by ordinary faith and practice. We take refuge in Christ Jesus and our Christian way of life repels these dark forces. But all of us must be vigilant.[2]

Four groups of persons seem to be the most vulnerable to demons. The first are the worldly who don't admit that demons exist. Therefore, they are reckless in associating with folks who practice dark magic, playing games and flirting with the occult either by reading satanic novels or watching films that specialize in this realm. The second at-risk group are the weak and non-thinking folk that blow here and there with the trends and cultural waves. The third group are the proficient who have developed spiritual powers through meditation and discipline. Spiritual pride first starts with the self but can gain strength and amazing power when aligned with dark forces. Again, we need to discern where the thought is coming from: God, self, or devil. Discernment is a gift of sight and is a fruit of purity of heart. Without it, the conflict with demons becomes more difficult because we lack the ability to discern. It is a vicious cycle! The fourth group are indiscriminate about spiritual energies. In the work with East-West dialogue, we hear authentic teachers from the Buddhist, Hindu, Islamic, and Taoist traditions warn Westerners of selective practices that stir levels of consciousness that are not properly prepared for by years of practice and training of the mind.

All four groups give us a healthy respect for the invisible. We know that some demons are neutral, are simply spirits in between worlds that need liberation from this world. They only serve to confuse us and strike fear in us, as in haunted houses. We also know that some demons can cluster in groups (coveys). These groups tend to form cults that engage people to use the forces of evil for their benefit: black magic, rituals, and gangs of evildoers. Demons tend to be attracted to folks who have pride as a major "thought." An "I can handle this" attitude is a mistake in judgment.

What should we do if we observe demons in ourselves or in those we love? There are ancient rituals of deliverance that can be done without any public dimension. Ministers who have been ordained and given the order of exorcism can administer the ancient approved rites. All priests have the faculty but not all have the grace to do this. It seems that "purity of heart" is required for a minister to cast out demons. Like the sacrament of reconciliation it's not hard to do the ritual. What is difficult is to free up the one who is infected. To people possessed by demons these combats with intelligent beings are not strange, nor spooky. The demons become companions, they are familiar, they feed a need for being something special and even flirting with risk in the lives of the possessed. A strange affinity toward evil develops. To do what is necessary to expel them goes against their inclination, because of a bond, an attachment, even a mingling of attitudes, goals, and mission. These people can "cast" these demons toward others as a weapon and so become quite strong in using spiritual forces.

In discernment, we sort out our thoughts to see if they are of God. God's way is toward peace. When we go God's way, consolation is the fruit. We can expect happiness. Benefits are bountiful and beyond expectations. Even the gross body feels lighter and moves more and more to subtle feelings, emotions, and an abiding disposition of wonder. God will not give us any affliction beyond our capacity.

Our energy naturally flows toward others. We feel that our intellectual powers are sharper. We understand Scripture. Our experience seems congruent with our expectations. Our memory improves. Equanimity replaces anxiety and worry. Our eyes are clear and we are helpful to others. We gradually find that sorting thoughts becomes easier and more natural. The grace to go toward God feels better than making choices for the self. Evil is repulsive, but we know ourselves well and we continuously practice ceaseless repentance. Here we know the safe harbor of compunction.

How can we know if our thoughts are from "the self"?

If the source of the thought is from the "self," we can notice a resistance or attraction that is thick with affect.

When we are acting from our selves we have amazing energy and feed on the benefits. The affliction of anger, especially, makes us feel righteously powerful.

The self has subtle, even cunning, punishments attached if we give in to it. I tell myself I'll get mad, depressed, anxious, or sick if I don't get my way about this. So the self-way sets up conditions for happiness. We even teach others how to gratify us! We coach; we ask for this or that praise. We feed into another's need to please us. We look good but do the right thing for the wrong reason. Life becomes all about my needs, my wants, my desires, and my ambitions. The self wants to be rewarded for being good and feels unjustly blamed if criticized, regardless of wrongdoing on the part of the self. Is there a way out of the self? Yes, discernment. We sort our thoughts and make choices to consent to God's way.

To have purity of heart we are called to return to our baptismal vows over and over again.

> Do I reject Satan? And all his works? And all his empty promises? Do I reject sin so as to live in the freedom of God's children? Do I reject the glamour of evil, and refuse to be mastered by sin? Do I reject Satan, father of sin and prince of darkness? Do I believe in God, the Father Almighty, creator of heaven and earth? Do I believe in Jesus Christ, his only Son, our Lord, who was born of the Virgin Mary, was crucified, died, and was buried, rose from the dead, and is now seated at the right hand of the Father? Do I believe in the Holy Spirit, the holy Catholic Church, the communion of Saints, the forgiveness of sins, the resurrection of the body, and life everlasting?
>
> After my profession of faith, the priest says: "God, the all-powerful Father of our Lord Jesus Christ, has given us a new birth by water and the Holy Spirit, and forgiven all our sins. May he also keep us faithful to our Lord Jesus Christ forever and ever."
>
> We say: "Amen." Then there is the blessing with the baptismal water.[3]

This is no empty, routine ritual but an anchor in our commitment to the spiritual journey. Once back in ordinary life we recommit ourselves to the inner work of renunciation. We resist doing self-motivated actions and strive to do selfless service and apostolic love. We continue our resolve to resist eating indiscriminately but use food mindfully whether we are feasting or fasting. We guard against lust (indiscriminate use of another's body) and relate reverently to another. We use things as if they are the sacred vessels of the altar. When anger rises, we return to our ceaseless prayer. When we are dejected, we look at the source of our dejection and take necessary action. If we need medication, we take it. If we need confession, we do it and make amends. If our hearts turn to stone and we want off the spiritual journey, we return to our cell and rededicate our daily life to doing manual labor. We discipline not only our thoughts but also our fantasy life and regard ourselves neither as worse nor better than others. In our own hearts we know how much we are in need of God's mercy.

Discernment in the Monastic Tradition

Discernment is the technical word for training our thoughts. The word *diakrisis* means to sort thoughts, see their source, and see how they allure us into one of the eight afflictions. To discern is to reason. It is part of the work of the second renunciation—making decisions that will enable us to follow our commitment to purity of heart.

Discernment also is part of the work of the first renunciation, aligning our exterior life with our interior life of virtue and fulfilling our baptismal promises. There is an urgency today to use discernment in making major decisions: vocational choices such as ordination to priesthood, final vows, marriage, or divorce. Some religious communities have a full-blown discernment process for election of a prioress or sending a nun on mission. Contemporary discernment may use such things as a database, networking, gathering statistical trend lines, and so forth. Some see discernment as a masculine model and are put off by it, preferring an intuitive process that skips the rational steps and depends on gut instincts and feelings of satisfaction. None of these forms, helpful as they may be, match the original tradition as taught by the elders. If we have a major decision to make, the following process might be helpful.

Notice our thoughts. Watch them rise and fall. Be aware how in any given day our thoughts and emotions shift, change, and go full circle. Do not be quick to act, since thoughts are fickle. We are not our thoughts. They come and they go. How can we trust them? When are they from God? From self or from the devil?

First, we seek God's help in the matter before us. We take the decision at hand to prayer, in the name of Jesus Christ or the Holy Spirit. The Our Father is the classic prayer that teaches us to ask for what we need. Prayer before, during, and after discernment is essential. In humble supplication we ask God not only for the wisdom to make the right choice but also for the grace to carry it out. We know in advance that God's way is the most beneficial for all concerned. Sorting is simply to remove one's self so that God's presence can spring up.

This process does not lead to quietism. It is hard work to sort, to receive, to be willing to see truth, and to do whatever it takes to follow the impulses of grace. Even though God can accomplish anything in a flash, the traditional steps are not arbitrary. They follow an orderly progression.

We know that the decision is in one sense "already made," since the answer is deep inside us. Our body, mind, and soul know what's best for us at this time. We only need to bring it to consciousness, sort through the options and find the energy (grace) of the moment.

There are seven steps in this process:

1. pray for enlightenment
2. sort our thoughts
3. virtually live the decision
4. look for a confirming sign
5. make the decision
6. ritualize the decision
7. guard our heart and watch our thoughts

Let's look at these steps, one by one.

Pray for enlightenment: St. Benedict says that whenever we begin any good work, we should beg earnestly in prayer for guidance about the right action and for the ability to carry out the consent. Here's where a pattern of prayer is the key ingredient. If we only pray when we have a major choice or a divide in the road, we will have a hard time praying at the moment of discernment. There are hints and road signs along our life's way, but what makes our life a way to God is having a practice of prayer. With training we can sense the impulses of grace and have already in place a willingness to follow God's call.

Sort our thoughts: We watch our thoughts as they rise and fall, sorting them into three buckets: thoughts toward self, toward God, and toward evil. We notice which thoughts weigh most heavily on our minds and eventually we see a pattern arise.

Virtually live the decision: We make a hypothetical decision based on the sorting in step two. For instance, it looks like it would be best for the family and me to move to Atlanta. . . . It seems that God has persistently called me to study medicine. . . . It seems like my business partner could be counted on for a new venture.

We take that tentative "choice" through the sorting process once again: is it toward self, toward God, or toward evil? We notice what this choice says. If possible, we manifest our thoughts to a wise elder. We simply lay out the thoughts, just as they seem to us. We do not gather more data. We try to verify whether indeed this choice that seems to be emerging is God's way for us. If the hypothetical choice still seems viable, we move to virtually live the decision.

We take the decision as a tentative given and "test" it. We put it on and act "as if" it is a decision that is final and to be implemented. Do I feel good about it? Usually if it is God's way, we feel a profound joy. Even if the decision has difficult consequences, the grace seems to be there to live with it.

Then we keep it in our consciousness "as if" the decision has been made for at least two weeks or more. Long enough to have several moods and to watch how we handle the climate of this decision.

While virtually living the decision, we may listen to other opinions and gather data but always consider that data in the light of the tentative decision. The reason not to invest too much weight on the feedback of others is because they are telling us what they would do. Their advice is coming through their thoughts. However, what they would do may or may not be helpful to us. To make this "as if" real, we talk to ourselves about the "as if" decision. It is best not to tell others that you've made the decision because they will then make the decision "a fact," and we will end up managing their grief or delight instead of knowing our thoughts. We continue to live the two weeks (or another prudent space of time) "as if" we were implementing the tentative decision.

Look for a confirming sign: We look for a sign from God that is convincing and supportive of the decision. We check our feelings and see if they are joyful and peace-filled. Even hard things should have a grace to match the difficulty. If there is no confirming sign, no consolation, or no ability to live in the decision "as if" it was real, then it is best to go back to step one and take up another "as if" decision and see if we have more confidence in an alternative option.

But if the "as if" brings joy, and there's grace to do it, and the confirming sign brings peace, then the decision is probably right.

Make the decision: We make the decision, putting it in concrete terms.

I've decided to take that job, or apply to St. Meinrad School of Theology, or move to Atlanta, or whatever the decision is. The decision is most helpful when it is clear, action-oriented, and I am the subject, the doer. Even if the decision is passive, "I will not move" or "I will not start graduate school," it is defining, with boundaries for implementation. A decision requires "the will to act." It represents a deliberate choice. It is one of the most awesome things a human can do: make choices and follow through as a co-creator with God. Notice the decision isn't a goal or an aspiration, but a deed to be done and done by me.

Ritualize the decision: Perhaps we light a candle, or write a letter confirming it, or call a friend. Mark the day on your calendar. Do the first step to implement it. In a sense, once the decision is made, all is already done— only not yet!

Guard our heart and watch our thoughts: Do what was envisioned. There's more to implementation than doing the work. Doing it includes the interior work of guarding our heart and watching our thoughts. This takes a lifetime. While implementing the decision, from time to time there will arise the thought that I wish I had not gone to St. Meinrad or moved to Atlanta or become a priest. At the earliest notice of that thought, dash it against the rock, Christ. We already know the value of guard of the heart and watchfulness of thoughts. Therefore, we consider our decision final and all "what ifs" as simply temptations that divide our heart and fragment our minds. We return to our ceaseless prayer.

You may say, "But what if I did make the wrong decision?" You made it in good faith and in prayer. If you should go now in another direction, God will make that evident in a significant way, so for the daily work of implementing this decision you need only attend to carrying out your resolve. This pattern of living a discerned life is the work of all of us, no matter what exterior form it may take. We should be at peace because we made the decision in good faith and God will show us a major sign if we are to change our decision. Our goal is purity of heart, lining up our external life so that it expresses our intentions to seek God in everyone and everything all the days of our life.

Let me lay out a scenario that may be helpful in our own discernment process. Question for discernment:

A move to Atlanta in order to take a promotion.

Step One: Prayer and fasting. My husband wants to take a job in Atlanta. "O Lord, come to my assistance, O God make haste to help me!" Spend time in prayer and turn completely to God as ask for guidance to go God's way.

Step Two: I sort my thoughts. . . .

> *Toward evil*: it would let me get more autonomy. No one knows me there. It would let me start over picking out a house, neighborhood, school, church, and I could set lesser goals, maybe soften my commitment to spiritual practices. I'm in a rut anyway and it's time to give myself some slack.
>
> *Toward self*: it would mean more money, prestige, opportunity, less stress, closer to his field of training, etc.
>
> *Toward God*: it could "up" my practices. We could live simpler. Choose our friends wisely. We could revise our goals, start setting realistic objectives for the sake of the family, and maybe I could put my personal goals into a secondary position.

Step Three: I make a decision to "live virtually." I gather data, but in my thoughts I act "as if" I have made the decision to move to Atlanta in July. I sort my thoughts again, while living in this "as if" provisional time.

> *Toward evil*: I have an old college friend in Atlanta. He's still where I was twenty years ago. It would be fun to have a night just with the old gang once in awhile. We drink a little too much when we are together, but everyone does that once in awhile.
>
> *Toward self*: this is good for my work and for me.
>
> *Toward God*: I have a chance at age forty to start over with my adult values. I will make family primary and budget my time as I budget money so that I have time to do spiritual work: prayer, reading, some involvement with a group of like-minded souls.

Step Four: I notice a confirming sign. We visited Atlanta and found a good house. It was affordable, available, and exactly what we need. Or the job offer came in and it will double my advancement compared to my work in Indianapolis. Or an event happened to one of the children and it would be best to move schools and even move out of the neighborhood to give him an advantage. The sign must be significant and fit the decision.

I notice a good, peace-filled feeling. Even if part of the move would be hard, there's an abiding grace that enables one to do tough things.

This is also the time I consult more folks and gather more data. I let all thoughts come and do "inner work" measured against the virtual decision. It is necessary for me to stay with the virtual decision because if I keep switching back and forth, my thoughts cannot go deep and the decision can't rise in a solid manner.

I'll ask my confidante to hear out my thinking on this: I'll call Uncle Luke and get some quality time with him and see if he thinks we are doing the right thing.

If the sorting of thoughts point to either selfishness or evil, if you can't live in the two weeks of virtual reality of implementing the decision, if there is no confirming sign, if there is no joy, peace, or consolation, if there's a vague discomfort and an abiding restlessness,, if there's an anxiety that's deep and abiding, then return to step one and make an alternate decision.

Step Five: Make the decision. We are moving.

Step Six: Ritualize the decision. We invite our folks over for dinner, offer a special prayer, and celebrate the decision.

Step Seven: Implement the decision. Make plans to move. I guard my heart and watch my thoughts. Every time a thought or a challenge emerges from the unconscious or from an outside source about the decision I dash it against the rock, Christ. It is just a temptation. For example: it's too much work to move; maybe we should wait till the children have finished school; I'll miss my friends; maybe we should just stay here; I'm not sure I'll get anything better or be any happier in Atlanta than I am in Indianapolis; I'll go ask the Smiths who just moved in.

Spiritual Direction

From the desert tradition we learn that the earliest form of spiritual direction was manifestation of thoughts to a wise elder. In the monastic tradition these elders responded with a word from Scripture. There were conferences in the monastic tradition speaking about the teachings, compiling them into Rules. For us who live in the third millennium we can only access these teachings through prayerful reading or by doing *lectio divina* on these inspired texts. But you might say, isn't there anyone with whom I can talk? How can I do the practice of manifestation of thoughts as the early monastics did?

We all feel the need of a spiritual director. That inclination is part of surrendering to God. It is also good for us to entrust ourselves to someone else in a visible manner. The joy of being heard is blessed.

From the view of the listener, the director: be welcoming and listen. Let the thoughts of the seeker come and refrain from engaging in conversation. Perhaps the seeker will need a few clarifying words to shift him or her away from commentary on her thoughts. Encourage straight talk. Refrain from problem solving. Let the words flow, session after session. Listen for which affliction is operative. At some point, when the seeker seems ready, ask questions about how he or she is attempting to deal with the affliction. Then offer the teaching about the affliction and a practice or tool to help the person control that affliction, for example, practice of the presence, the emptiness practice, or the Little Way.

Then, session after session, listen to how the practice is going. Lead them into doing *lectio* with a spiritual classic that teaches that practice, for example, *He and I* for colloquy practice or *The Cloud of Unknowing* for emptiness practice. The listener teaches the theory behind the practice and helps the seeker to remove any obstacles to the practice and to develop a positive way to use the tool, for example, setting up a "cell" in their home. The listener accepts the sacred trust of confidence and promises to pray for the seeker.

The best preparation for the listener is *lectio divina* and personal practice, using the tools as needed. The elder, as we see from the desert tradition, is a tool herself, a tool for the training. When we need someone like this, God provides. If the student is ready, the teacher appears.

From the view of a seeker: the selection of an elder requires finding someone who doesn't have the same afflictions I have, or if she had them at one time, now uses tools to keep them before God's mercy. The process of manifesting thoughts is simply to say what comes to mind. Name the obstacles to prayer, simply and humbly. If possible, refrain from analysis and commentary. Just let the words flow and notice the thoughts. Take the time required to slow down your thoughts. Shift down a gear in order to see one thought at a time. If you are confused about which thoughts are from God, self, or evil, ask your elder. If you are stuck in a loop of circular thinking, lay each thought out as if you were shaking flour from your hands. Share your thoughts about motivations and intentions. If you have secrets, test them by sharing them. It's not the content of the secret that is important as much as it is the nature of secrets to control thoughts and escalate into dramas. Clarify questions about practice. Share insights from *lectio*. Begin with prayer and end with a blessing.

The Limitations of Tools

Though tools are helps on the way, there are at least ten ways they can get in the way, so we must be careful when we use them. Perhaps the biggest problem is to mistake the means for the end. Tools are simply the boat we use to reach the shore. We then must leave them in exchange for the object of our desire: God. We know we are attached to a tool when we are rigid, when we are not willing to shift, to change, to modify, to let go, to lay aside the tool when it's clear that it is in the way of our progress toward God. If we have a reluctance to follow the impulse of grace, then the tool and not God controls our response.

A tool also can be good for another, but not for us. Each of us is called in a specific and individualized way. We can't imitate another, no matter how much we admire that person. Our relationship with God determines our vocation. With our call to be in relationship with God comes the context or the "way" of living, vocation. That we discussed in the earlier chapters on discernment.

We know that in and of themselves tools are neutral, neither good nor bad. What determines their benefit is how they lead us to a deeper relationship with God. A tool appropriate when I was a child may no longer empower me to scatter the darkness or gather myself in recollection. We must have a radical openness to embrace a tool and use it as long as it is useful, but then to let it go for the sake of another method or practice that better suits us now. We can't insist on a practice being normative for us the whole of our lives, nor normative for everyone with whom we reside. Tools are useful for a time, for a person, even for a group, but when they no longer effect the desired change they should be laid aside. Since we are often not the best judges of ourselves, an elder can be of assistance in this discernment.

Tools, while specific for a time or a person, must also be used with our full attention and for as long as they are required to make God's way visible. When we are in training, learning about a particular tool, we do not have the option to mix and match tools at will. Each tool has it's own dynamics. If we are learning to practice recollection, that is not the time to expand our senses in free-fall association. If we are sharing our every thought in colloquy, that isn't the time to practice emptiness as in *The Cloud of Unknowing*. We can't image and not image at the same time.

How does one know? What is the right effort? When do we discard a tool? When are we overconfident about it? When are we just being faint-hearted? Finding answers to these questions is the role of spiritual direction. We lay out our thoughts to a wise elder. She listens not only to our thoughts but also to our motivations and intentions. She asks us to look at the fruits evident in our everyday life. If we don't have an elder, we do *lectio* with wise texts, beginning with Scripture and the inspired writings of our Christian saints.

We should distrust protracted absorption, as it is often torpor, and be alert to phenomena that come through conditioned senses. God doesn't need extraordinary visions, locutions, raptures, and ecstasy to be a sacred presence. We should take no delight in any spiritual experience that takes us away from apostolic love for others and compunction for ourselves, being on guard against "lights" that heighten our powers and capture our ego. Seeing moving objects, reading hearts, foretelling the future, being smart beyond our ability, seeing lights and colors, all can be a detour away from an authentic relationship with God.

Tools are tricky also because they work on a human level. The discipline and concentration of the mind can produce the thought or feeling of holiness. Most of the saints report no such feelings. Holiness or sanctity can only be measured by the spiritual senses, so we have reason to distrust ordinary thoughts and feelings that return to the self, such as, "What a good girl am I." When we do or do not do what we ought to because of what others might think or what we think of ourselves, we are victims of vainglory. This being said, there's the converse danger that we discard a tool precisely because it is working on our behalf and we fear the consequences of conversion.

Probably the greatest problem when selecting, using, or discarding a tool is to think we have anything to do with the value of a tool. Tools are means of grace. Grace is given to us freely, as is the impulse toward using a particular tool. We receive it and use it humbly in a spirit of detachment. We hold our hands empty, our hearts warmed, and our minds ready for clarity. God does the rest. We are sometimes active and eager and at other times passive and waiting, but we are always respectful and pliant to the subtleties of grace.

At the risk of negating our attraction to all the tools presented in this book it might be helpful to name the downside of each tool:

• Guard of the heart may play into the human impulse to move toward hardness of heart. When we refrain from engaging with others, we keep ourselves from interacting with them. While guard of the heart prevents evil from entering our heart, it should not cancel opportunities for us to be compassionate to others.

• Watchfulness of thoughts helps us to notice how our thoughts come and go and when they allure us into consent. The only downside to watchfulness of thoughts is if one were prone to scrupulosity or over-concerned about her spiritual welfare. We need to watch and pray, not worry and fret.

• Fasting has a downside if we become so food conscious that we don't consider others, especially the cooks and those who prepare foods for us. Fasting also is a choice and is tempered by feasting and hospitality. The biggest downside is becoming judgmental.

• Dreams can absorb us. Either fear of the future or anxiety about the past may rob us of the present moment. In one sense entrance into the dream world collapses time and space. It's a mysterious adventure. If we get too sure of what our dreams mean, we could be misusing their helpful indicators. The best advice is to check dreams and take them lightly. Let them be instructive for the now. If we become worrisome or anxious, this tool is tricking us into self-consciousness.

• Ceaseless repentance requires maturity. If we understand all actions as moral decisions, the results may be more guilt than we can bear. A good fruit of ceaseless repentance is restored relationships and right order in our lives.

• Ceaseless prayer is a practice that holds our wandering thoughts in check. Fear of the unknown or our dark mysterious shadow side still needs to be faced. Ceaseless prayer is not a tool to thwart truth.

• Manual labor sometimes needs to be done for the sake of others and our spiritual practice has to be laid aside. We might be called to do mental work or to sit with the dying. Our active side might feel bored or restless without the rhythmic use of our hands. Manual labor is just one tool. Without question obedience takes precedence. Another sign that manual labor is an obstacle and not a tool leading us toward God is if there are indications of overwork. We become too busy and the affliction of greed is "at work," not God.

• The cell is for the sake of God and is not a place to hide.

• Vigils can be self-willed and not aligned with one's strength or the duty of the day. What good are they if we are awake for the dawn but in a torpor all day?

• Manifestation of thoughts to a wise elder has all sorts of pitfalls. There may be transference or counter-transference. We could manifest our thoughts to an unwise elder who should not be trusted. Or the tool may simply degenerate into self-centered whining and "woe is me" sessions. Silence is always better than mere chatter.

• The twelve steps of humility when done with faith and wholeheartedly offer no problem that I can see. Our culture will present resistance to this tool so that few of us practice it enough to see how rapidly humility takes us to Christ.

• Ministry as selfless service has no downside unless we resent the cost.

• Sharing at the common table must be discerned. Not everything should be shared.

• The Jesus Prayer and Prayer of the Heart, when done as directed in the inspired writings of the Christian East, give only grace. The one caution is that, in saying only the name of Jesus, a reverence must accompany it because there is a very thin line between adoration and blasphemy.

• Emptiness practice can lead us to avoid engagement in life. I find the most authentic practitioners of *The Cloud* also use a form of the Jesus prayer.

• Practice of the presence at first seems easy, but then it "backdoors" into living a life with such attentiveness that there's a major striving which is at once serious and playful. But there's grief when one finds out that one's free-fall thoughts are now in the service of one's contemplative life. No more fantasy.

• Abandonment to the present moment has no down side that I can see unless it masks an avoidance of taking responsibility, but then the present moment will reveal if one is sincerely living with total faith.

• Colloquy is only dangerous if we don't practice it enough to be good listeners to Christ's subtle ways.

• Recollection becomes tricky between its active and its passive phases. Right effort must accompany the practice. Read St. Teresa's *Way of Perfection* and her *Interior Castle* for her teachings and warnings about this practice.

• Redemptive suffering is very tricky. We need guidance to practice it. It can slip sideways into self-destructive patterns.

• The Little Way is only dangerous if we misunderstand how selfless we must be and begin to feel how special we are just being nothing.

• Discernment is our friend. If we do it in good faith it has no problems. In fact, without it we are doomed. However, discernment can also be the hardest trick of all. A good corrective is to continuously live in a spirit of *lectio divina* where the spiritual senses of Scripture communicate with our own spiritual senses. The literal meanings of the text and the literal choices we need to make have been made countless times before our lifetime. The Scriptures store wisdom that can be retrieved in our days. This is no magic tool that would have us open the Bible and throw a dart on a page. The daily receptive absorption of God mediated through this sacred text is the greatest help to discernment.

• Probably the biggest trick would be to think we have renounced our former way of life and have simply just taken it into the next renunciation, and the next. We can actually think we have renounced all for God, at God's prompting, and it is all simply an intellectual choice and not a response to God's presence.

So all these tools are tricky. We first see them one way and then another. Therefore, we should have reservations about our own actions and rely on tradition and on elders. A sound practice of these tools within a community is a healthy teacher, too. But when we know that we've been called in faith and that God has graced us with the ways to respond, our hearts will be eager to follow the truth that is planted, rooted, and tended in the garden of our soul.

CONCLUSION
When Tools Don't Matter

Just as "thoughts matter" so also do "tools matter" for the spiritual life. We need help in tending the garden of our souls. But after some practice we see that we use the same tools to control our thoughts no matter what the content of those thoughts. For example, when we are angry we return to our ceaseless prayer. If we are greedy for this or that, we return to our ceaseless prayer. The content of the thought really doesn't matter. So, too, the tools are sometimes interchangeable since they do the same thing. We return to God instead of to our thoughts. It really doesn't matter which tool we use. Sometimes, by God's grace, we don't need any tool at all. This work isn't labor, but leisure since we'd rather be no place else! God's grace prevails; our spiritual senses spring up and catch the subtleties of taste, sound, sight, touch, and smell. Eventually we discover, with freedom and love, that tools don't matter after all! What matters is our Heart's Desire!

NOTES

Introduction

1. All references to Cassian's works are to the following editions: *The Institutes,* edited by Boniface Ramsey, O.P. (New York: Newman/Paulist Press, 2000), and *The Conferences,* edited by Boniface Ramsey, O.P. (New York: Newman/Paulist Press, 1997). References are to work (*Inst., Conf.*), book or conference number, chapter, and section. Page numbers have not been given.

Chapter 1: Thoughts and Tools

1. See Jeremy Driscoll, O.S.B., *The Mind's Long Journey to the Holy Trinity: The "Ad Monachos" of Evagrius Ponticus* (Collegeville, Minn.: Liturgical Press, 1993). See also Thomas Spidlik, *The Spirituality of the Christian East: A Systematic Handbook,* trans. A. P. Gythiel (Kalamazoo, Mich.: Cistercian Publications, 1986).

2. Spidlik, *The Spirituality of the Christian East,* p. 32, quoting Theophane the Recluse: "The Spirit is the soul of the soul."

3. Evagrius Ponticus, *The Praktikos and Chapters on Prayer,* trans. John Eudes Bamberger, O.C.S.O. (Kalamazoo, Mich.: Cistercian Publications, 1972). Bamberger notes in his introduction (p. 7) that, according to Irenee Hausherr, Evagrius did not necessarily invent this system. For a lucid discussion of the eight thoughts, see John Climacus, *The Ladder of Divine Ascent,* trans. Colm Luibheid and Norman Russell (New York: Paulist Press, 1982), p. 62.

4. Taken from letters to Archbishop Daniel Buechlein and used with permission.

5. Taken from conversations between Father Thomas Keating and the author.

6. Guigo II, *The Ladder of Monks and Twelve Meditations,* trans. Edmund Colledge, O.S.A., and James Walsh, S.J. (Garden City, N.Y.: Image Books, 1978; Kalamazoo, Mich.: Cistercian Publications, 1982).

7. See chap. 6 below for the practice of emptiness; also *The Cloud of Unknowing and the Book of Privy Counseling,* ed. William Johnston, S.J. (Garden City, N.Y., 1973).

8. See Columba Stewart, *Cassian the Monk* (New York: Oxford University Press, 1998), chap. 1.

Chapter 2: Afflictions

1. Mary Margaret Funk, *Thoughts Matter* (New York: Continuum, 1998), p. 81.

2. Ibid., p. 82.

3. Evagrius Ponticus, *Praktikos,* p. 18.

4. Funk, *Thoughts Matter,* p. 119.

Chapter 3: Negative Tools

1. *Philokalia: The Complete Text,* vols. 1–4, compiled by St. Nikodemus of the Holy Mountain and St. Makarios of Corinth, trans. and ed. G. E. H. Palmer, Philip Sherrad, and Kallistos Ware (London: Faber and Faber, 1979–1995).

2. *Purity of Heart in Early Ascetic and Monastic Literature,* ed. Harriet A. Luckman and Linda Kuzler, O.S.B. (Collegeville, Minn.: Liturgical Press, 1999), p. 157.

3. Irenee Hausherr, S.J., *Spiritual Direction in the Early Christian East* (Kalamazoo, Mich.: Cistercian Publications, 1990), p. 157.

4. John Climacus, *The Ladder of Divine Ascent,* pp. 181–182.

5. Evagrius Ponticus, *Praktikos,* introduction, pp. xxxix–xl.

6. Ibid., pp. 31 and 33–34.

7. For further teaching on dreams, see Martin Israel, *The Spirit of Counsel: Spiritual Perspectives in the Counseling Process* (Wilton, Conn.: Morehouse-Barlow, 1983).

8. Robert A. Johnson, *Inner Work: Using Dreams and Active Imagination for Personal Growth* (San Francisco: HarperCollins, 1986).

9. Kurt Stasiak, O.S.B., *A Confessor's Handbook* (New York: Paulist Press, 1999).

10. Irenee Hausherr, *Penthos: The Doctrine of Compunction in the Christian East,* trans. Anselm Hufstader (Kalamazoo, Mich.: Cistercian Publications, 1982), pp. 17–18.

11. Irma Zaleski, *The Way of Repentance* (New York: Continuum, 1999).

Chapter 4: Positive Tools

1. See Isaiah 55:11 and Acts 4:12.

2. See Psalm 70.

3. See Jean Pierre de Caussade, *Abandonment to Divine Providence,* trans. John Beevers (Garden City, N.Y.: Image Books, 1975).

4. *RB 1980, The Rule of St. Benedict in Latin and English with Notes,* ed. Timothy Fry, O.S.B. (Collegeville, Minn.: Liturgical Press, 1981), p. 229.

5. Ciarán Ó Sabhaois, O.C.S.O., editorial "In Praise of Manual Prayer," *Hallel* 26/1 (2001):2. *Hallel: A Review of Monastic Spirituality and Liturgy* is published twice yearly by the Region of the Isles of the Cistercian Order of the Strict Observance, St. Joseph Abbey, Roscrea, Co. Tipperary, Ireland. hallel@msjroscrea.ie.

6. Thomas Merton, *Contemplation in a World of Action* (Garden City, N.Y.: Doubleday, 1971).

7. Charles Cummings, O.C.S.O., *Monastic Practices* (Kalamazoo, Mich.: Cistercian Publications, 1986), p. 133.

8. Everett Fox, *The Book of Moses: A New Translation with Introductions, Commentary, and Notes* (New York: Schocken Books, 1995), p. 323.

9. *RB 1980,* pp. 203–207.

10. *Hallel* 26/1 (2001), p. 44.

11. For the authoritative teaching on manifestation of thoughts, see Hausherr, *Spiritual Direction in the Early Christian East.*

12. Irenee Hauscherr, S.J., *Penthos: The Doctrine of Compunction in the Christian East* (Kalamazoo, Mich.: Cistercian Publications, 1982), p. 71.

13. Ibid., p. 72.

14. *RB 1980,* p. 185.

15. Stasiak, *A Confessor's Handbook,* p. 9.

16. See Hausherr, *Spiritual Direction.*

17. *RB 1980,* p. 185.

Chapter 5: Social Tools

1. *RB 1980,* pp. 191–203.

2. Ibid., p. 199.

Chapter 6: Prayer Tools

1. Theophan the Recluse describes this warming of the heart. This can be found in *The Art of Prayer: An Orthodox Anthology,* compiled by Igumen Chariton of Valamo, trans. E. Kadloubovsky and E. M. Palmer, ed. Timothy Ware (London: Faber and Faber, 1966).

2. *Writings from the Philokalia on Prayer of the Heart,* trans. E. Kadloubovsky and G. E. H. Palmer (London: Faber and Faber, 1951).

3. *The Cloud of Unknowing and the Book of Privy Counseling,* ed. William Johnston, S.J. (New York: Image Books, 1973).

4. Ibid., p. 47.

5. Ibid., pp. 48–49.

6. Ibid., p. 55.

8. Ibid. See pp. 152–153.

9. Ibid., pp. 144–146.

10. *The Little Way of St. Thérèse of Lisieux: Readings for Prayer and Meditation,* compiled by John Nelson (Liguori, Mo.: Liguori Publiations, 1997), p. 17.

11. *RB 1980,* p. 295.

12. Pierre Descouvemont and Helmuth Nils Loose, *Thérèse and Liseux,* trans. Salvatore Scurbia, O.C.D., and Louise Pambran (Toronto: Novalis, 1996), p. 55.

13. Ibid., p. 78.

14. Ibid., p. 190.

15. Ibid., p. 294.

16. Ibid., p. 174.

17. Ibid., p. 216.

18. Ibid., p. 132.

19. Ibid., p. 122.

20. Ibid., p. 224.

21. Jean Pierre de Caussade, S.J., *Self-Abandonment to Divine Providence,* trans. Algar Thorold (Rockford, Ill.: Tan Books, 1987), p. 33.

22. Brother Lawrence, *The Practice of the Presence of God,* trans. Robert E. Edmonson (Brewster, Mass.: Paraclete Press, 1985), p. 94. Quote at the end of paragraph is from ibid., 36.

23. Ibid., p. 68.

24. Ibid., p. 82.

25. Ibid., p. 101.

26. Ibid., pp. 106–8 and 114–115.

27. Ibid. p. 115.

28. Gabrielle Bossis, *He and I,* trans. and condensed by Evelyn M. Brown (Quebec: Médiaspaul, 1985), from the French *Lui et Moi* (Paris: Beauchesne, 1969).

29. Ibid., p. 142.

30. Ibid., p. 55.

31. Ibid., p. 21.

32. *The Collected Works of Teresa of Avila,* vol. 2, trans. Kieran Kavanaugh, O.C.D., and Otilio Rodriguez, O.C.D. (Washington, D.C.: Institute of Carmelite Studies, 1980), p. 140.

33. Ibid., p. 147.

34. Ibid., p. 140.

35. Ibid., p. 141.

36. Ibid.

37. Ibid., p. 319.

38. Ibid., p. 143.

39. Ibid.

40. Ibid., pp. 147.

41. Ibid., p. 148.

42. Ibid., pp. 148–149.

43. Ibid., p. 270.

44. Ibid.

45. Ibid., p. 271.

46. Ibid.

47. Ibid., pp. 272–273.

48. Ibid., pp. 273–274.

49. Ibid., p. 369.

50. Ibid., pp. 276–278.

51. Ibid., p. 450.

52. Attachment (desire) is the belief that something you do not have will make you happy, content, peaceful.

53. Anthony de Mello, S.J., *De Mello Satellite Retreat,* taped at Fordham University, New York, 1986. Produced and distributed by We and God Spirituality Center, Jesuit Hall, St. Louis University, St. Louis, Mo., 1989.

54. To develop this idea I read the following letters of Paul: 1 and 2 Corinthians, Galatians, Philippians, and 1 Thessalonians. At this point I have read no commentaries or other works on Paul and his writings. I wanted to begin by coming fresh to Paul's let-

ters. I will look at the secondary literature in the future to get their insights and the benefit of their knowledge, because I believe that a sound idea can always stand up to scrutiny. Of course, it is possible that scholars may disagree with my insights. I want to stress that this is not a study of these letters; it is a look into this idea.

55. Adapted from the teaching of De Mello on the tape mentioned in note 52.

Chapter 7: Tools of Discernment

1. Evagrius Ponticus, *Praktikos,* pp. 4–10.
2. Israel, *The Spirit of Counsel,* pp. 80–94.
3. *Living with Christ, Triduum 2000* (Champlain, N.Y.: Novalis, 2000), pp. 96–97.

SELECT BIBLIOGRAPHY

1. Ancient Texts

Antony the Great, St. *The Letters of Saint Antony the Great*. Trans. Derwas J. Chitty. Fairacres, Oxford: Sisters of the Love of God Press, 1975.

Athanasius. *The Life of Anthony and the Letter to Marcellinus*. Trans. Robert C. Gregg. Classics of Western Spirituality. New York: Paulist Press, 1980. This influential fourth-century work could be considered the first handbook in the Christian ascetical tradition.

Benedict. *RB 1980: The Rule of St. Benedict in Latin and English with Notes*. Ed. Timothy Fry, O.S.B. Collegeville, Minn.: Liturgical Press, 1981. A modern English translation of Benedict's sixth-century Rule with the Latin text, explanatory notes, topical essays, indexes, and a Latin concordance. A small English-only edition without the scholarly additions is also available.

____. *Benedict's Rule: A Translation and Commentary*. Trans. Terrence Kardong, O.S.B. Collegeville, Minn.: Liturgical Press, 1996. A detailed line-by-line analysis of the Rule; includes background essays and both English and Latin texts.

Bernard of Clairvaux. *Bernard of Clairvaux, A Lover Teaching the Way of Love: Selected Spiritual Writings*. Ed. M. Basil Pennington. Classics of Western Spirituality. New York: New City Press, 1997. This collection includes St. Bernard's commentary on St. Benedict's twelve steps of humility.

Cassian, John. *Conferences*. Trans. Colm Luibheid. Classics of Western Spirituality. New York: Paulist Press, 1985. A translation of nine of Cassian's twenty-four conferences, including the important ninth and tenth conferences on prayer.

____. *The Conferences*. Trans. Boniface Ramsey, O.P. Ancient Christian Writers: no. 57. New York: Newman/Paulist Press, 1997. Cassian's dialogues with the great desert masters on the practice of the spiritual life.

____. *The Institutes*. Trans. Boniface Ramsey, O.P. Ancient Christian Writers: no. 58. New York: Newman/Paulist Press, 2000. Cassian's record of the rules of monastic life in Egypt and lessons on struggles against the eight thoughts.

_____. *Making Life a Prayer: Selected Writings of John Cassian.* Ed. Keith Beasley-Topliffe. Nashville: Upper Room Books, 1997. A small collection of Cassian's writing from the *Institutes* and *Conferences.*

_____. *The Works of John Cassian.* Trans. Edgar C. S. Gibson. A Select Library of Nicene and Post Nicene Fathers: Second Series. Vol. 11. 1894. Ed. Phillip Schaff and Henry Wace. Peabody, Mass.: Hendrickson Publishers, 1994. This early English translation omits *Institute* 6 and *Conferences* 12 and 22.

Climacus, John. *The Ladder of Divine Ascent.* Trans. Colm Luibheid and Norman Russell. Classics of Western Spirituality. New York: Paulist Press, 1982. A seventh-century instruction on the ascetic life and practice, this work had a profound influence on the development of the monastic life in the Eastern Church, especially the hesychast (Jesus Prayer) movement.

The Desert Fathers: Translations from the Latin. 1936. Trans. Helen Waddell. Ann Arbor, Mich.: University of Michigan Press, 1957. Portions of the lives and sayings of the desert fathers and mothers translated from the *Verbum Senorium.*

Evagrius Ponticus. *The Mind's Long Journey to the Holy Trinity: The "Ad Monachos" of Evagrius Ponticus.* Trans. Jeremy Driscoll, O.S.B. Collegeville, Minn.: Liturgical Press, 1993. A collection of 137 proverbs intended for sustained meditation on the spiritual path to God.

_____. *The Praktikos and Chapters on Prayer.* Trans. John Eudes Bamberger, O.C.S.O. Cistercian Studies Series; no. 4. Kalamazoo, Mich.: Cistercian Publications, 1972. A translation of two works by Evagrius: *The Praktikos* deals with the eight thoughts and the ascetic life; *Chapters* contains 152 sentences on prayer.

Gregory of Nyssa, St. *From Glory to Glory: Texts from Gregory of Nyssa's Mystical Writings.* Ed. Jean Danielou, S.J., and Herbert Musurillo, S.J. New York: Charles Scribner's Sons, 1961.

Journeying into God: Seven Early Monastic Lives. Trans. Tim Vivian. Minneapolis: Fortress, 1996. The stories of seven Greek and Coptic monastics; each life is introduced with historical and theological background.

Lives of the Desert Fathers: The Historia Monachorum in Aegypto. Trans. Norman Russell. Cistercian Studies Series; no. 34. Kalamazoo, Mich.: Cistercian Publications, 1981. An account of the monastic life encountered in a journey through Egypt at the end of the fourth century.

The Life of Saint Pachomius and His Disciples. Trans. Armand Veilleux. Vol. 1 of Pachomian Koinonia. Cistercian Studies Series; no. 45. Kalamazoo, Mich.: Cistercian Publications, 1980. The story of Pachomius, founder of monastic communal (cenobitic) life characterized by shared labor and liturgy.

Palladius. *The Lausiac History.* Trans. Robert T. Meyer. Ancient Christian Writers Series; no. 4. New York: Paulist Press, 1965. A fifth-century description of desert fathers and mothers in Egypt, Palestine, Syria, and Asia Minor.

The Sayings of the Desert Fathers: The Alphabetical Collection. Trans. Benedicta Ward, S.L.G. Cistercian Studies Series; no. 59. Kalamazoo, Mich.: Cistercian Publications, 1975. The only English translation of the most complete version of the *Apophtegmata Patrum: Alphabetical Series,* a Greek collection in which the sayings of each father are grouped under his name and arranged alphabetically.

Seeking a Purer Christian Life: Sayings and Stories of the Desert Mothers and Fathers. Ed. Keith Beasley-Topliffe. Nashville: Upper Room Books, 2000.

The Wisdom of the Desert. Comp. Thomas Merton. New York: New Directions, 1960. A collection of Merton's favorite sayings from the *Verbum Senorium* (Latin) collection of desert father sayings.

The Wisdom of the Desert Fathers: Apophthegmata Patrum from the Anonymous Series. Trans. Benedicta Ward, S.L.G. Kalamazoo, Mich.: Cistercian Publications, 1975. A partial translation of the Greek collection *Apophthegmata Patrum: Anonymous Series;* the sayings are arranged by subject.

2. The Desert Tradition and Practice: Modern Reflections

Allen, Diogenes. *Spiritual Theology: The Theology of Yesterday for Spiritual Help Today*. Cambridge: Cowley Publications, 1997. An examination of the spiritual disciplines and practices of the past, with a focus on the traditional threefold path.

Bianchi, Enzo. *Praying the Word: An Introduction to Lectio Divina*. Cistercian Studies Series; no. 182. Trans. James W. Zona. Kalamazoo, Mich.: Cistercian Publications, 1998.

Bondi, Roberta. *To Love as God Loves: Conversations with the Early Church*. Philadelphia: Fortress Press, 1987. An exploration into the spiritual insights of the ancient monastic tradition, including the eight thoughts.

____. *To Pray and Love: Conversations on Prayer with the Early Church*. Minneapolis: Fortress Press, 1991. Lessons from the desert masters on the practice of prayer.

Casey, Michael. *Sacred Reading: The Ancient Art of Lectio Divina*. Liguori, Mo.: Triumph Books, 1995.

____. *Toward God: The Ancient Wisdom of Western Prayer*. Rev. ed. Liguori, Mo.: Triumph Books, 1996. An exploration into the nature of prayer and guidance for its practice derived from the teaching of the early church.

Clement, Oliver. *The Roots of Christian Mysticism: Text and Commentary*. Trans. Theodore Berkeley, O.C.S.O., and Jeremy Hummerstone. New York: New City Press, 1995. Carefully chosen texts and reflections revealing the depth of the mystery of Christ as lived in the early Christian centuries.

Cummings, Charles, O.C.S.O. *Monastic Practices*. Cistercian Studies Series; no. 75. Kalamazoo, Mich.: Cistercian Publications, 1986. Reflections on the meaning and observance of traditional monastic practice.

Dreuille, Mayeul de, O.S.B. *The Rule of St. Benedict and the Ascetic Traditions from Asia to the West*. Trans. Mayeul de Dreuille, O.S.B. and Mark Hargreaves, O.S.B., England: MPG Books, 2000.

Funk, Mary Margaret, O.S.B. "Cassian's Three Renunciations." *Benedictines* LI:1 (Summer 1998): 42–47.

____. *Thoughts Matter: The Practice of the Spiritual Life*. New York: Continuum, 1998. A summary of Cassian's teaching on the renunciation of the eight afflictive thoughts.

Gruen, Anselm. *Heaven Begins Within You: Wisdom from the Desert Fathers*. Trans. Peter Heinegg. New York: Crossroad, 1999. An exploration of desert spirituality as contending with the passions as the way to God.

Hausherr, Irenee, S.J. *Spiritual Direction in the Early Christian East*. Cistercian Studies Series; no. 116. Trans. Anthony P. Gythiel. Kalamazoo, Mich.: Cistercian Publications, 1990.

Keating, Thomas. *Invitation to Love: The Way of Christian Contemplation*. New York: Continuum, 1996. A conceptual framework for the practice of prayer is presented; Anthony of Egypt is used as a paradigm of the spiritual journey.

____. *Fruits and Gifts of the Spirit*. New York: Lantern Books, 2000.

____. *Open Mind, Open Heart: The Contemplative Dimension of the Gospel*. New York: Continuum, 1986. A guide to contemplative prayer that addresses the experience of thoughts and attentiveness.

Masini, Mario. *Lectio Divina: An Ancient Prayer That Is Ever New*. Trans. Edmund C. Lane, S.S.P. New York: Alba House, 1998.

Mayers, Gregory. *Listen to the Desert: Secrets of Spiritual Maturity from the Desert Fathers and Mothers*. Liguori, Mo.: Triumph Books, 1996. Interpretations of desert sayings through the lens of modern and transpersonal psychology.

Merton, Thomas. *The Climate of Monastic Prayer*. Cistercian Studies Series; no. 1. Kalamazoo, Mich.: Cistercian Publications, 1973. An exploration of monasticism and the nature of prayer.

____. *Contemplation in a World of Action*. New York: Doubleday, 1971.

A Monk of the Eastern Church. *The Prayer of Jesus: Its Genesis, Development, and Practice in the Byzantine-Slavic Religious Tradition*. Trans. A Monk of the Western Church. New York: Desclee Company, 1967.

Nouwen, Henri. *The Way of the Heart*. 1981. San Francisco: Harper Collins, 1991. Reflections on the sayings and wisdom of the desert tradition as a source of nourishment and strength for contemporary ministry.

A Priest of the Byzantine Church. *Reflections on the Jesus Prayer: A Phrase-by-Phrase Analysis of "The Prayer of the Heart."* Denville, N.J.: Dimension Books, 1978.

Purity of Heart in Early Ascetic and Monastic Literature. Ed. Harriet A. Luckman and Linda Kulzer, O.S.B. Collegeville, Minn.: Liturgical Press, 1999.

Salvail, Ghislaine. *At the Crossroads of the Scripture: An Introduction to Lectio Divina*. 1994. Trans. Paul C. Duggan. Boston, Mass.: Pauline Books and Media, 1996. This small book is a practical introduction to *lectio divina* and includes comments on the biblical and liturgical roots of this practice.

Stinissen, Wilfrid. *Nourished by the Word: Reading the Bible Contemplatively*. Trans. Joseph B. Board, Liguori, Mo.: Liguori Publications, 1999. A simple guide to *lectio divina* which includes discussion of the spiritual nature of the biblical text and an explanation of the fourfold meaning of Scripture illustrated with scriptural texts.

3. Background Reading

Bouyer, Louis. *The Spirituality of the New Testament and the Fathers*. San Francisco: Harper Collins, 1963. A comprehensive study of the spirituality of the first Christian centuries.

Burton-Christie, Douglas. *The Word in the Desert: Scripture and the Quest for Holiness in Early Christian Monasticism*. New York: Oxford University Press, 1993. A study of how Scripture formed the lives of the early desert Christians.

Israel, Martin. *The Spirit of Counsel*. Wilton, Conn.: Morehouse-Barlow, 1983. Integrated presentation on discernment including deliverance from demons.

Johnston, William, S.J. *Arise, My Love*. Maryknoll, N.Y.: Orbis, 2000. A wise collection from a wise man about mystical paths.

Kierkegaard, Søren. *Purity of Heart Is to Will One Thing.* Trans. Douglas V. Steere. New York: Harper and Row, 1938.

Leclerq, Jean, O.S.B., *The Love of Learning and the Desire for God: A Study of Monastic Culture.* 1957. Trans. Catherine Misrahi. New York: Fordham University Press, 1961. A review of the development of the monastic milieu ordered toward the monk's search for God.

McGinn, Bernard. *The Presence of God: A History of Western Christian Mysticism.* 3 vols. to date. New York: Crossroad, 1991–. An extensive theological and historical appraisal of mystical experience in Western Christianity; five volumes are projected.

Maloney, George. *Gold, Frankincense, and Myrrh: An Introduction to Eastern Christian Spirituality.* New York: Crossroad, 1997. An introduction to the theology and masters of the Eastern church from the fourth to eighth centuries.

Osborne, Arthur. *Ramana Maharshi and the Path of Self-Knowledge.* York Beach, Me.: Samuel Weiser, Inc., 1970.

Spidlik, Thomas, S.J. *The Spirituality of the Christian East: A Systematic Handbook.* Trans. Anthony P. Gythiel. Cistercian Studies Series; no. 79. Kalamazoo, Mich.: Cistercian Publications, 1978. An orderly treatment of themes in the Eastern spiritual tradition, incorporating writings ranging from antiquity to present day.

Stasiak, Kurt, O.S.B. *A Confessor's Handbook.* New York: Paulist Press, 1999.

Stewart, Columba. *Cassian the Monk.* New York: Oxford University Press, 1998. A thorough discussion of Cassian's teaching on the theory and practice of monastic asceticism.

The Study of Spirituality. Ed. Cheslyn Jones, Geoffrey Wainwright, Edward Yarnold, S.J. New York: Oxford University Press, 1986. A one-volume survey of the history of spirituality with articles representing the Anglican, Free Church, Orthodox, and Roman Catholic traditions.

Tolstoy, Leo. *The Wisdom of Humankind.* Trans. Guy de Mallac. Ada, Mich.: CoNexus Press, 1999.

Underhill, Evelyn. *Mysticism: A Study in the Nature and Development of Man's Spiritual Consciousness.* 1911. New York: Oneworld Publications, 1999. A classic; this pioneering work studies the transcendent realm of religious experience.

Yogananda, Paramahansa. *Man's Eternal Quest.* Los Angeles: Self-Realization Fellowship, 1975.

Selected Bibliography for Prayer Practices

THE JESUS PRAYER AND PRAYER OF THE HEART

The Art of Prayer: An Orthodox Anthology. Comp. Igumen Chariton of Valamo. Trans. E. Kadloubovsky and E. M. Palmer. Ed. Timothy Ware. London: Faber and Faber, 1966. A collection of texts on prayer compiled by a Russian monk in the course of his quest for prayer in the monastic life.

Goettmann, Alphonse and Rachel. *Prayer of Jesus—Prayer of the Heart.* Trans. Theodore and Rebecca Nottingham. Greenwood, Ind.: Inner Life Publications, 1996. This guide to the Jesus Prayer written by an Orthodox priest and his wife includes some biblical and historical details, as well as counsel on the practice of the Jesus Prayer.

Hausherr, Irenee, S.J. *The Name of Jesus.* Trans. Charles Cummings, O.C.S.O. Cistercian Studies Series; no. 44. Kalamazoo, Mich.: Cistercian Publications, 1978. A study of the names of Jesus used by early Christians and the historical development of the Jesus Prayer.

Matus, Thomas. *Yoga and the Jesus Prayer Tradition: An Experiment in Faith.* Ramsey, N.J.: Paulist Press, 1984. A comparison of the spiritual disciplines of the Jesus Prayer and tantric yoga.

A Monk of the Eastern Church (Lev Gillet). *The Jesus Prayer.* Rev. ed. Crestwood, N.Y.: St. Vladimir's Seminary Press, 1987. An introduction to the history and classic teaching of the Jesus Prayer, with some advice on its practical use.

____. *On the Invocation of the Name of Jesus.* 1949. Springfield Ill.: Templegate, 1985. This is a fuller treatment of the practice of the Jesus Prayer than what is found in *The Jesus Prayer* (see above).

Philokalia: The Complete Text, vols. 1–4. Comp. St. Nikidemos of the Holy Mountain and St. Makarios of Corinth. Trans. and ed. G.E.H. Palmer, Philip Sherrard, and Kallistos Ware. London: Faber and Faber, 1979–1995. An anthology of the spiritual writings of the early fathers. This is the primary source for all teaching on the Jesus Prayer.

____. *Writings from the Philokalia on Prayer of the Heart.* Trans. E. Kadloubovsky and G. E. H. Palmer. London: Faber and Faber, 1951. Selected portions of the *Philokalia* compiled from the Russian version.

The Pilgrim's Tale. Ed. Aleksei Pentkovsky. Trans. T. Allan Smith. Classics of Western Spirituality. New York: Paulist Press, 1999. A translation of the *Way of the Pilgrim* from the earliest known version. The introduction details the intricate history of the text.

Sophrony, Archimandrite. *On Prayer.* Trans. Rosemary Edmonds. Crestwood, N.Y.: St. Vladimir's Seminary Press, 1998. Part I is a collection of writings on prayer and the spiritual life. Part II deals with the theory and practice of the Jesus Prayer.

Stinissen, Wilfrid. *Praying the Name of Jesus: The Ancient Wisdom of the Jesus Prayer.* Trans. Joseph B. Board. Liguori, Mo.: Ligouri Publications, 1999. Part I is a reprint of *On the Invocation of the Name of Jesus,* by Lev Gillet, a Monk of the Eastern Church (see above). Part II follows the development of the Jesus Prayer and gives guidance for practice of the prayer.

Theophan the Recluse. *The Spiritual Life and How to Be Attuned to It.* Trans. Alexandra Dockham. Forestville, Calif.: St. Herman of Alaska Brotherhood, 1995. This volume is compiled from letters on the spiritual life written by St. Theophan, who also translated the *Philokalia* into Russian.

Ware, Kallistos. *The Orthodox Way.* Rev. ed. Crestwood, N.Y.: St. Vladimir's Seminary Press, 1995. A popular account of the Orthodox Church's doctrine and life, which includes teaching on theology and prayer.

____. *The Power of the Name.* Oxford: SLG Press, 1974. A concise introduction to the Jesus Prayer and its practice by the Orthodox Bishop of Diokleia (Great Britain).

The Way of a Pilgrim and the Pilgrim Continues His Way. 1965. Trans. R.M. French. San Francisco: Harper Collins, 1991. The story of a nineteenth-century Russian pilgrim who seeks to "pray without ceasing."

The Way of a Pilgrim and the Pilgrim Continues His Way. Trans. Helen Bacovcin. New York: Doubleday, 1978. Another translation of the pilgrim's chronicle.

Zaleski, Irma. *Living the Jesus Prayer.* New York: Continuum, 1997. This 56-page book contains brief meditations on the Jesus Prayer by a modern practitioner.

EMPTINESS—THE CLOUD OF UNKNOWING

The Cloud of Unknowing. Trans. James A. Walsh, S.J. Classics of Western Spirtuality. New York: Paulist Press, 1981. A modern version with an extensive introduction and many notes.

The Cloud of Unknowing. Ed. Evelyn Underhill. 1912. Rockport, Mass.: Element, 1997. A literal rendering of the text which keeps close to the original Middle English.

The Cloud of Unknowing and other Works. Trans. Clifton Wolters. London: Penguin Books, 1961, 1978. A very readable version. Three other works by the author of *The Cloud* are included in this single volume.

The Cloud of Unknowing and The Book of Privy Counseling. Ed. William Johnston. New York: Image, 1973.

Cooper, Austin, O.M.I. *The Cloud: Reflections on Selected Texts*. New York: Alba House, 1989. These meditations place the *Cloud of Unknowing* in the wider context of biblical and Christian spiritual tradition.

Gregory of Nyssa. *The Life of Moses*. Trans. Abraham J. Malherbe and Everett Ferguson. Classics of Western Spirituality. New York: Paulist Press, 1978. An account of the soul's ascent to God in the darkness of unknowing.

Johnston, William, S.J., *The Mysticism of the Cloud of Unknowing*. New York: Desclee, 1967.

Llewelyn, Robert. *All Shall Be Well*. New York: Paulist Press, 1982. Includes a clear and practical discussion of the Cloud of Unknowing as a spiritual path.

Pseudo-Dionysius. *The Complete Works*. Trans. Colm Luibheid. Classics of Western Spirituality. New York: Paulist Press, 1987. This scholarly volume contains a primary source of apophatic "negative theology."

The Pursuit of Wisdom and Other Works by the Author of the Cloud of Unknowing. Trans. James A. Walsh, S.J. Classics of Western Spirituality. New York: Paulist Press, 1988. The remaining known works of the author of *The Cloud of Unknowing*, translated by James A. Walsh, S.J. (see above).

THE LITTLE WAY

Ahern, Patrick. *Maurice and Thérèse: The Story of a Love*. New York: Doubleday, 1998. The correspondence between St. Thérèse and a struggling seminarian is supplemented with biographical notes and interpretations of St. Thérèse's teaching.

Descouvemont, Pierre, and Helmuth Nils Loose. *Thérèse and Liseux*. Trans. Salvatore Scurbia, O.C.D., and Louise Pambran. Toronto: Novalis, 1996. A lavishly illustrated account of Thérèse's childhoood and life in Carmel.

St. Thérèse de Lisieux. *Her Last Conversations*. Trans. John Clarke, O.C.D. Washington, D.C.: ICS Publications 1977. Contains St. Thérèse's final interviews collected by her sisters during the last months of St. Thérèse's life.

Thérèse de Lisieux. *Daily Readings with St. Thérèse of Lisieux*. Ed. Michael Hollings. Springfield Ill.: Templegate Publishers, 1986. A small anthology of St. Thérèse's writing arranged for daily reading.

————. *General Correspondence*. Trans. John Clarke, O.C.D. 2 vols. Washington, D.C.: ICS Publications, 1982, 1988. A critical edition of all the letters written by St. Thérèse. These are accompanied by all the letters from her correspondents and other letters elucidating upon her life and thought.

____. *The Poetry of St. Thérèse of Lisieux*. Trans. Donald Kinney, O.C.D. Washington D.C.: ICS Publications, 1996. A critical edition of all the poems written by St. Thérèse according to the autographs and different copies. This is the only English translation of the complete original texts.

____. *The Prayers of St. Thérèse of Lisieux*. Trans. Aletheia Kane, O.C.D. Washington, D.C.: ICS Publications, 1997. A critical edition of St. Thérèse's prayers.

____. *Story of a Soul: The Autobiography of St. Thérèse of Lisieux*. 3rd ed. Trans. John Clark, O.C.D. Washington, D.C.: ICS Publications, 1996. This is St. Thérèse's main work. This edition is translated from the original manuscript written by St. Thérèse.

____. *The Little Way of St. Thérèse of Lisieux: Readings for Prayer and Meditation*. Comp. John Nelson. Liguori, Mo.: Liguori Publications, 1997. Excerpts from St. Thérèse writings and sayings are interwoven with passages from Scripture and *The Imitation of Christ* by Thomas à Kempis, whose writing was a source of inspiration for St. Thérèse.

ABANDONMENT TO DIVINE PROVIDENCE

Caussade, Jean Pierre de. *Abandonment to Divine Providence*. Trans. John Beevers. Garden City, N.Y.: Image Books, 1975. This translation is made from an extensive and later revision of the original manuscript which had been put together by the Visitation nuns.

____. *The Sacrament of the Present Moment*. Trans. Kitty Muggeridge. San Francisco: Harper Collins, 1989. This translation is made from the original manuscript compiled from de Caussade's letters and conferences and circulated privately by the Visitation nuns after de Caussade's death.

____. *Self-Abandonment to Divine Providence*. 1959. Trans. Algar Thorold. Rockford, Ill.: Tan Books, 1987. This volume contains a translation of de Caussade's revised manuscript and his letters.

____. *Spiritual Letters of Jean-Pierre de Caussade*. Trans. Kitty Muggeridge. Wilton, Conn.: Morehouse-Barlow, 1986. De Caussade's sensitivity and simplicity as a spiritual teacher are evident in this collection of his letters.

____. *A Treatise on Prayer from the Heart*. Trans. Robert M. McKeon. St. Louis: Institute of Jesuit Sources, 1998. A translation of de Caussade's lesser known work; a guidebook on prayer; includes an introduction to his teaching and theology.

Francis de Sales. *Finding God Wherever You Are*. Ed. Joseph F. Power, O.S.F.S. New Rochelle, N.Y.: New City Press, 1993. An anthology of de Sales's spiritual writing selected from the introduction to the *Devout Life* and *Treatise on the Love of God*, as well as his letters of spiritual direction.

Francis de Sales and Jane de Chantal. *Letters of Spiritual Direction*. Trans. Péronne Marie Thibert, V.H.M. Comp. Wendy M. Wright and Joseph F. Power, O.S.F.S. Classics of Western Spirituality. New York: Paulist Press, 1988. De Cassaude refers frequently to de Sales and de Chantal in his own writing. This volume of their letters of direction reveal the warmth and humanity of their counsel, which de Caussade also possessed.

John of the Cross. *The Collected Works of St. John of the Cross*. Rev. ed. Trans. Kieran Kavanaugh, O.C.D., and Otilio Rodriguez, O.C.D. Washington, D.C.: ICS Publications, 1991. All of the works of St. John of the Cross are in this volume.

THE PRACTICE OF THE PRESENCE OF GOD

Brother Lawrence of the Resurrection. *Daily Readings with Brother Lawrence.* Intro. Robert Llewelyn. Springfield, Ill.: Templegate Publishers, 1985. There are many versions of Brother Lawrence's work in print. In this edition the Conversations and Letters of Brother Lawrence are arranged for daily reading and meditation.

____. *The Practice of the Presence of God.* Trans. Robert J. Edmonson. Ed. Hal M. Helms. Brewster, Mass.: Paraclete Press, 1985. This edition includes Brother Lawrence's Letters, Conversations, and Spiritual Maxims, as well as two biographical sketches written shortly after his death.

____. *Writings and Conversations on the Practice of the Presence of God.* Ed. Conrad DeMeester, O.C.D. Trans. Salvatore Scurbia, O.C.D. Washington, D.C.: Institute of Carmelite Studies, 1994. This is the scholarly, critical translation of Brother Lawrence. In addition to all of the texts listed in the previous entry, this volume includes relevant historical and theological background.

COLLOQUY

Bossis, Gabrielle. *He and I.* 1969. Trans. Evelyn M. Brown. Sherbrooke, Que.: Editions Médiaspaul, 1985. The words of Christ to a modern French laywoman.

Cousins, Ewert. "The Humanity and the Passion of Christ." In *Christian Spirituality: High Middle Ages and Reformation.* Ed. Jill Raitt. New York: Crossroad, 1987. 375–91. This essay traces the development of devotion to the humanity of Christ.

A Monk of the Eastern Church (Lev Gillet). *A Day with Jesus.* Trans. A Monk of the Western Church. New York: Desclee Co., 1964. A monologue addressed to Christ during a day spent in union with him.

____. *Jesus, a Dialogue with the Saviour.* 1963. Trans. A Monk of the Western Church. West Newton, Mass.: Educational Services, Diocese of Newton, 1990. Brief meditations which are dialogues with Christ, filled with gospel scenes and images.

Rahner, Karl, S. J. *Watch and Pray with Me.* New York: Herder and Herder, 1966. Two poignant meditations addressed to Christ in his Passion.

Thomas à Kempis. *The Imitation of Christ.* Trans. William Creasy. Notre Dame: Ave Maria, 1989. In a brief introduction, the translator clearly defines the historical, literary and theological issues which face the modern reader of this beloved spiritual classic. The translator seeks to present the text so that it may be read and experienced in the same way as its fifteenth century readers.

Thomas à Kempis. *The Imitation of Christ.* 1955. Ed. Harold C. Gardiner, S. J. New York: Image, 1989. A modern version based on the English translation made by Richard Whitlord around the year 1530.

Thomas à Kempis. *The Imitation of Christ.* Trans. Ronald Knox and Michael Oakley. 1959. South Bend, Ind.: Greenlawn Press, 1990. This translation is intended to be as clear, direct, and colloquial as it is in its original language.

Two Listeners. *God Calling.* Ed. A. J. Russell. 1935. New York: Jove Books, 1978. The words of Christ revealed to two Englishwomen in the 1930's.

RECOLLECTION

Culligan, Kevin, O.C.D., Mary Jo Meadow, O.C.D.S., and Daniel Chowning, O.C.D. *Purifying the Heart: Buddhist Insight Meditation for Christians*. New York: Crossroad, 1994. A guide to Christian insight meditation which incorporates Buddhist meditation practice into the Carmelite tradition of contemplative prayer, especially as taught by John of the Cross.

Judy, Dwight H. *Embracing God: Praying with Teresa of Avila*. Nashville: Abingdon Press, 1996. A presentation of meditative prayer practice derived from St. Teresa's writings.

Morello, Sam Anthony, O.C.D. *Lectio Divina and the Practice of Teresian Prayer*. Washington, D.C.: ICS Publications, 1995. This pamphlet explains St. Teresa of Avila's principles of meditation and applies them to the practice of Lectio divina.

The Soul's Passion for God: Selected Writings of Teresa of Avila. Ed. Keith Beasley-Topliffe. Nashville: Upper Room Books, 1997. A small anthology of St. Teresa's writing on prayer.

Teresa of Avila. *The Collected Works of St. Teresa of Avila,* vols. 1–3. Trans. Kieran Kavanaugh, O.C.D., and Otilio Rodriguez, O.C.D. Washington, D.C. : ICS Publications, 1976–1985. Vol. 1: The Book of Her Life, Spiritual Testimonies, Soliloquies. Vol. 2: The Way of Perfection, Meditation on the Song of Songs, The Interior Castle. Vol. 3: The Book of Her Foundations, Constitutions, On Making the Visitation, A Satirical Critique, Response to a Spiritual Calling, Poetry. Modern translations of St. Teresa's works, these critical editions contain helpful background and introductory information.

____. *The Interior Castle*. Trans. Kieran Kavanaugh, O.C.D., and Otilio Rodriguez, O.C.D. Classics of Western Spirituality. New York: Paulist Press, 1979. Written at the end of her life, this is St. Teresa's most thorough and orderly account of the spiritual life.

____. *The Letters of St. Teresa of Jesus,* vols. 1–2. Trans. and Ed. E. Allison Peers. London: Sheed and Ward, 1980. A collection of over four hundred letters written by St. Teresa of Avila. This edition is no longer in print, ICS Publications plans to publish a new translation of her letters.

____. *The Way of Perfection: A Study Edition*. Trans. Kieran Kavanaugh, O.C.D., and Otilio Rodriguez, O.C.D. Ed. Kieran Kavanaugh, O.C.D. Washington, D.C.: ICS Publications, 2000. Written for her nuns as a guide to prayer, this study edition of St. Teresa's *The Way of Perfection* includes an introduction, commentary, notes, discussion questions, and glossary.

CEASELESS REPENTANCE

Hausherr, Irenee, S.J. *Penthos: The Doctrine of Compunction in the Christian East*. Trans. Anselm Hufstader, O.S.B. Cistercian Studies Series; no. 53. Kalamazoo, Mich.: Cistercian Publications, 1982. A scholarly study of the place of heartfelt compunction in the teaching and spirituality of the early church and the Eastern monastic tradition.

Symeon the New Theologian. *The Discourses* Trans. C.J. de Cantanzaro. Classics of Western Spirituality. New York: Paulist Press. 1980. This prominent Greek spiritual writer emphasizes the importance of repentance and tears.

Ward, Benedicta, S.L.G. *Harlots of the Desert: A Study of Repentance in Early Monastic Sources.* Kalamazoo, Mich.: Cistercian Publications, 1987. Early monastic stories which speak of God's presence and work in the lives of the sinful who repent.

Zaleski, Irma. *The Way of Repentance.* New York: Continuum, 1999. A guide to the practice of repentance both as natural response to our separation from God and as an experience of God's mercy.

Grace Suffering

Chodron, Pema. *Start Where You Are,* Boston: Shambhala Publications. 1994. A guide to Tibetan Buddhist teachings which use life's difficulties and problems to awaken our hearts.

_____. *The Wisdom of No Escape.* Boston: Shambhala Publications, 1991. A series of talks given during a one-month meditation retreat which includes instruction on the tonglen practice of receiving in pain and suffering and sending out compassion.

Fiand, Barbara. *Prayer and the Quest for Healing.* New York: Crossroad, 1999. Explores humanity's shared experience of brokenness and need for continuous conversion and the ongoing process of individual, communal, and cosmic healing.

Israel, Martin. *The Pain That Heals.* 1981. New York: Continuum, 2001. This book asserts the creative potentiality of suffering and looks for a wider ministry of healing than that designed merely to smooth out life's difficulties.